HINLO

ELIZABETH FRY

BRITAIN'S SECOND LADY ON
THE FIVE-POUND NOTE

CHANADON PUBLICATIONS LTD
PO Box 37431, London N3 2XP
www.chanadon.co.uk

Published by Chanadon Publications Ltd 2004
Based on a version by Friedrich Muller 1954 and the diaries of Elizabeth Fry.

ISBN   0-9541973-5-6

135798642

A catalogue record of this book is available from the British Library

Formatted by Brewin Books Ltd, Studley, Warks.
Printed and bound by Janet 45, Bulgaria

Jacket imagery provided by the Mary Evans Picture Library, London
Designed by Alistair Brewin

ELIZABETH FRY

BRITAIN'S SECOND LADY ON THE FIVE-POUND NOTE

DENNIS BARDENS

Foreword by John Mackrell

Chanadon Publications Ltd
London

Elizabeth Fry.

Courtesy of Mary Evans Picture Library

CONTENTS

ACKNOWLEDGMENTS

Great thanks go to Mrs Joyce Wischuff both for the unstinting help she gave to the author, Dennis Bardens, in the last years of his life and for her wholehearted support in the preparation of this book. Many others have undertaken research for this project or helped through their commitment to it. Among these are Rosemarie Cockayne, Julia Couchman, Maggie MacDougall and Angie Schiano. Their efforts are much appreciated. Eudora Pascall of Friends House has been kindness itself in offering assistance.

John Mackrell's introduction needs no fanfare here, its exceptional qualities being self-evident, so we record with gratitude how willingly, speedily and efficiently he devoted himself to this project. Adrian Smith took an interest in the welfare of the book and indeed of its author that went beyond his brief. Melissa Zanmmiller has become a tower of strength from the point she joined the editorial team.

We gratefully acknowledge the considerate assistance of the Mary Evans Picture Library in supplying the illustrations.

FOREWORD

Dennis Bardens breathes life into Elizabeth Fry, as few biographers have done before him. She is no easy subject. Elizabeth Fry is infuriating in her very perfection. 'We long to burn her alive,' wrote the Reverend Sydney Smith in 1821, because 'examples of living virtue disturb our repose and give birth to distressing comparisons.'[1] Yet the real test of a biographer, which Dennis Bardens passes so spectacularly, is to present his ascetic heroine just as convincingly as the reprobates, whom we generally prefer, because they are often more like ourselves. Even the sun has its spots and it is true, that if you take a microscope to Elizabeth's character, there is something forced about her steely perfection. Years of unchallenged leadership caused Elizabeth to be something of a *mulier fortis*, to borrow a term favoured by Catholic priests for an outspoken woman. The niece, who accompanied her on a tour of the Continent, noted in her diary that it was 'droll to see how Aunt makes *all* work, whoever they may be'. Perhaps, she was too fond of luxury and her contacts with 'the great of the earth', though these were used invariably to further her work of reform.[2] Muted criticisms are all that can be held against her. Elizabeth's genuine humility appears again and again in her voluminous diaries, where she was her own sternest critic.

Elizabeth's personality, as Dennis Bardens brings out so clearly, was by far her greatest asset. Elizabeth had one quality, which practically every other reformer in nineteenth-century Britain – and indeed today – lacked. She was totally non-judgemental. The calming effect of Elizabeth's presence among 'the wild beasts' of popular imagination was not derived from magical enchantment, as contemporaries seemed to think. The reason was altogether simpler. Elizabeth Fry was the first person in the lives of many of these women to accept them as they were, treat them with respect and to refrain from all condemnation. That is the secret of successful psychotherapy today and was virtually unknown in Elizabeth Fry's time. Her approach worked instantaneously, as many of the female prisoners had been abused since birth and were treated as dangerous vermin by judges, gaolers, chaplains and society at large. Such an attitude was all the more galling to them, as some were innocent and many had committed only minor crimes of theft, to which hunger had driven them. The genuine concern for their physical and emotional well-being touched a chord in many of these women, which nobody else had ever reached. The way in which Elizabeth identified with them by speaking simply of 'we' and 'us' helped to forge a unique bond between her and her charges. Elizabeth's words as reported in *The Hangman* in 1845 have the same power to move us today:

"I am come to serve you, if you will allow me," said Elizabeth Fry. She then went on to express her sympathy for them, and offer them hope, that they might improve their condition. She did not say a word about the crimes they had committed, nor reproach them. She came to comfort, not to condemn.[3]

It is only necessary, under Dennis' guidance, to follow Elizabeth into Newgate Prison, to feel the miraculous calm and hope she brought to all around her. The same is true, perhaps most movingly of all, when the reader stands beside Elizabeth on the deck of the convict ship, *Maria*, while the women deportees clutched their little bundles and bags, with all the items so thoughtfully collected by Elizabeth, for their long and hazardous journey to Australia.

How did Elizabeth Fry become the charismatic prison reformer? It isn't easy, as Dennis Bardens underlines, to understand how Elizabeth, who in childhood was fearful, delicate and withdrawn, transformed herself into a heroine. Elizabeth was the first to recognise her debt to her warm-hearted and understanding family. In her memoirs, she recounts how she used to withdraw from play with her sisters, to their obvious hurt and was, in her own words 'disposed to a spirit of contradiction' and 'had a reputation for being obstinate'. Elizabeth's mother, despite having another eleven offspring, seems to have given her 'dove-like Betsy' a disproportionate amount of time and encouragement[4]. After her mother's death, when Elizabeth was twelve, her father was indulgence itself. On her whim to visit London as a teenager, he furnished her with letters of introduction to his friends and accompanied her there himself. Nor did he object to part of his house being turned into a school for 'Betsy's imps', eventually numbering an astonishing seventy-six. In later life family bonds remained strong. When Elizabeth's husband, Joseph, was on the verge of bankruptcy, Elizabeth was able to farm out some of her children to her sisters. When older, Elizabeth grew close to her brother Joseph, who accompanied her on her Continental journeys.

While there is no denying the warmth of family affection, Elizabeth seems to have had an unhappy childhood and to have been depressed by loneliness in the midst of her often more ebullient eleven siblings. She relates that she was terrified of the dark, of water and even of death. 'My childlike wish was, that two large walls might crush us all together, that we might die at once, and thus avoid the misery of each other's death. I seldom, if I could help it, left my mother's side, I watched her when asleep with exquisite anxiety to check that she was still breathing.' Did these death-wishes hint, as a Freudian might surmise, that Elizabeth wished to escape a claustrophobic upbringing, as she would do shortly, through her surprise request some years later to visit London? At all events, Elizabeth was haunted by her sense of her own inferiority to her sisters, Catherine and Rachel. 'I was considered and called very stupid' and she added that 'having the name of being stupid, really tended to make me so.' And saddest of all, Elizabeth could not bring herself to confide in anyone.[5] These inner demons, as much as religious conviction itself, seem to have propelled her forward in her public career to help others. That may partly explain the driven nature of her life, the rising at 4 am. to attend to household duties at Mildred Court and to work often for sixteen hours a day. Was it because she lacked real intimacy that Elizabeth always seems to have been happiest when she was in the company of those to whom she ministered? The repeated self-recriminations in her journal suggest that the love so many gave to Elizabeth she could not give herself. That does not at all detract from the heroic work Elizabeth did for others, but it may help to explain an apparent lack of warmth towards those who were neither her charges nor close relatives.

The early nineteenth century was probably the only period in English history when a penal reformer of Elizabeth Fry's stamp could have made her mark. In earlier times an aspiring female reformer would have been treated as a disturber of the peace, fortunate if only consigned to her husband for a sound whipping. Wife-beating in the eighteenth century was permitted, if not actually encouraged, by the authorities, though according to the ruling of an indulgent judge, the stick should be no thicker than a man's thumb. A few decades later women visitors were virtually debarred from entry into prisons, where men were increasingly jealous of exercising control.

The eighteenth-century state, to view the situation in broad terms, was wedged between the monarchical Stuart despotism of the seventeenth century and the bourgeois bureaucratic state of the later nineteenth century. By Continental standards, the central government was incredibly weak. The Government was essentially a pawn of the aristocracy, whose authority was based in the shires. The balance of power between centre and periphery may be measured by the existence of no more than nineteen staff to service both the Home and Foreign Offices, while Poor Relief, workhouses and prisons were all administered locally[6]. Elizabeth Fry, therefore, did not have to deal with an obstructive civil service, as she would today, but could gain access to individual prisons with comparative ease.

Was the climate of opinion in the late eighteenth century important in seconding the prison reforms of Elizabeth Fry? While it is notoriously difficult to measure intellectual influences, they afforded her some support. Prison reform was junior partner to the campaign for the abolition of the slave trade. The ultimate success of the slave abolitionists under Elizabeth's brother-in-law, Sir Thomas Fowell Buxton, can only have given her own campaign a boost. Buxton did, in fact, give her substantial support in 1818 in his powerful, *An Inquiry whether crimes and misery are produced or prevented by our present system of prison discipline,* in which he described her methods at length with approval. Jeremy Bentham's writings on penal reform earlier in the century had considerable impact on the educated public. The frequently published *Treatise on Crimes and Punishments,* of Cesare Beccaria, who argued passionately that savage punishments and most of all the death penalty were ineffectual, as well as repugnant to humanity, also won converts. More important than abstract ideas in promoting penal reform, was John Howard's *State of the Prisons in England and Wales,* which by exposing conditions in the prisons stirred the public's conscience.

Elizabeth Fry drew important support from her fellow Quakers. The principles of the founder of *The Society of Friends,* George Fox (1624-1691) remained the touchstone of Quakerism, well into the nineteenth century and for some longer still. Fox's conversion arose from his experience of what he believed to be direct contact with God. That provoked in his mind the conviction of man's equality, since 'no man can honestly claim the guidance of God for himself without recognising it in others.' Fox's wife, Margaret Fell (1614-1702) somewhat to the founder's chagrin, pushed his principle still further, to include women. The belief that 'the inner light' made all men equal in the eyes of God shaped Quaker behaviour in all human relations. Special distinctions and honours, which set one man above another, were seen as a slight to God, to whom honour alone was due. Hence the persecution of Quakers who refused to bare their heads before figures of authority and on other matters of conscience, such as refusing to swear oaths, pay tithes and insistence on worshipping separately. Between 1652 and the Glorious Revolution of 1688 hundreds, sometimes thousands, of Friends were in prison each year.[7] Memories of wrongful imprisonment of their own members barely a hundred years earlier must surely have aroused the sympathies of Elizabeth Fry and her circle for prisoners in her own day. Elizabeth herself often made a point of reminding people that some of the prisoners, at the very least those remanded before trial, were innocent, just as her forbears had been.

If faith were the basis of Quaker belief, self-discipline and tight organisation made the Friends a powerful force in the world. The Meetings were models of working democracy. There was complete respect for the individual and recognition of real equality, irrespective of social and economic status. A deep love, reminiscent of that famous among the early Christians, pervaded relationships between Quakers right into at least the nineteenth century. Terms of endearment to other Friends run through their correspondence. Master and servant would ride together to the Meeting and discuss its business on equal terms.[9] Inter-marriage, required of Friends on pain of exclusion, further tightened the bonds among them, as did attendance at Meetings, often across considerable distances and also the large number of itinerant preachers. As a result, a large proportion of Friends knew one another, as shown, for instance, during the course of the grand tour of England and Wales, which John Gurney took with his family, including Elizabeth. Throughout, it is apparent from Dennis Bardens' colourful account, they always stayed with other wealthy Quaker families.

No group, however cohesive, would have had any purchase on Britain's ruling class, were they not themselves members of it. The rise in society of the Quakers is as mysterious as their influence in high circles is widely attested. In the seventeenth century, Friends appear to have been mainly craftsmen and artisans. By the early nineteenth century they numbered industrials, merchants and bankers, with leverage in high society and government. The Quakers, denied positions as dissenters in Church and State, and by excluding themselves on grounds of conscience from any calling that resorted to violence, such as the armed forces and the judiciary were limited in choice of career. Agriculture was effectively barred, because at least in the early days they lacked capital for the purchase of land. That left them manufactures, trade and for a few, science and medicine. For commerce, however, Quakers seemed to be particularly well suited by their religion. The Friends' egalitarianism made for excellent relationships with employees. Further, their sober life-style encouraged them to plough back profits into their businesses. Disapproving of worldly ostentation, Quakers were not tempted to abandon business for the social respectability of the landed gentry. Further, their religion encouraged a spirit of inquiry, which may account for their industrial inventions, especially in the iron and mining industries, and also perhaps for their astuteness in banking, the other area in which they excelled. At any rate, the Quakers formed a powerful network with considerable influence among the ruling classes. Elizabeth Fry, therefore, had the social connections that gained her entry to the country's prisons and even access to Parliament and the Queen.

To mount a campaign to help female prisoners, Elizabeth Fry needed other women to help her. Elizabeth's disciples would hardly have been forthcoming without the rapid growth of feminism during the eighteenth century. The main stimulus came from the evangelicals, who also had a direct influence on the Quakers, not least on Elizabeth herself. The evangelicals, originally within the Church of England and only later as Methodists a separate church, emphasised Original Sin and the utter depravity of mankind. They lauded the 'feminine virtues' of meekness, gentleness, temperance and chastity, to the point where women were prized for their 'latent moral superiority'. Providence, suggested William Wilberforce, the leading evangelical, had so divided the role of the sexes, that men in the public sphere, daily encountering the temptations of worldly life, should be sustained by that 'more favourable disposition to religion in the female sex'.[9] Whether moved by virtue or flattery, women worked in support of evangelical causes with such effect that by 1819 the British and Foreign Bible Society had about 350 female associations with some 10,000 women active. To these should be added numerous female groups, engaged in other forms of social work from campaigning for the abolition of slavery to care of the destitute. Women had not only found some of their natural vocations but had also learnt solidarity through work together as women free from men[10].

Women's entry into politics had already taken place in the women's sections, which supported the abolition of the slave trade. It was a sign of the increasing politicisation of women that in 1780 the first female debating society, *La Belle Assemblée,* opened and received favourable reviews from a leading paper, *The Morning Chronicle.* The women were reported as questioning the values of their society, demanding better education for women and reacting strongly to the current state of political affairs. Although La Belle Assemblée closed later in the same year, apparent victim of the backlash to the Gordon Riots, other female initiatives would follow, notably feminine support for the Chartists.[11] In *The Times that Try Men's Souls*, Maria Weston Chapman in 1837 saucily taunted her political masters:

Confusion has seized us, and all things go wrong,
The women have leaped from 'their spheres,'
And instead of fixed stars, shoot as comets along,
And are setting the world by the ears!

They've taken a notion to speak for themselves,
And are wielding the tongue and the pen;
They've mounted the rostrum; the termagent elves,
And – oh horrid! are talking to men![12]

Elizabeth Fry has been denied recognition as a true pioneer of feminism. It seems to be assumed – for it is rarely stated – that because she handed out Bibles and religious tracts, she was no liberator of women, but rather a purveyor of Karl Marx's 'opium of the people'. In short, Elizabeth Fry often appears to be pilloried for failing to conform to the preferred stereotype of the humanitarian heroine. Yet, on closer inspection, this difference is more one of style, than of substance. Always opposed to the death penalty, Elizabeth was certainly no 'Christian' in the style set by the Archbishop of Canterbury. In 1810, he voted with six other bishops in the House of Lords against a bill that would have abolished sentence of death for stealing five shillings from a shop[13]. While it is true that Elizabeth Fry collaborated with the evangelicals in their campaign against slavery, she rejected their belief in Original Sin and of fallen human nature. Her Quaker belief that there is an 'inner light' – a spark of the divine – in every human being is surely akin to humanism. Although Elizabeth Fry wished ultimately to lead the female prisoners to belief in a Christian God, her immediate concern – and the one that made its deepest impression on the female prisoners – was their physical and mental well-being. Forcing consciences, least of all in religion, was totally opposed to her Quaker beliefs.

On the face of it, a more serious charge is that Elizabeth was so irremediably middle-class that she was ill-fitted to bring freedom to the working-class women, to whom she ministered. Even that accusation has little substance. Elizabeth was undoubtedly middle-class and accepted, like almost everyone else of the time, that the class system was a necessary part of English society. More importantly – and this is of cardinal importance from a feminist viewpoint – Elizabeth identified herself with the female prisoners, in a way which effectively removed class barriers. While reading out Romans, she pointedly explained that the Apostle meant 'our sex as well', as if to draw the sting from St Paul's misogyny. A heart-felt reference to 'one common bond of sisterhood' again underlines her feminism.[14] Yet, the best proof of all lay in Elizabeth's efforts to galvanise women Quakers to participate with her in prison work. She was quite clear in her *Observations on the Visiting, Superintendence, and Government of*

Female Prisoners of 1827 that women should fulfil a public role in society:

> It is a dangerous error to suppose that the duties of females end here [in domesticity]. Their gentleness, their natural sympathy for the afflicted, their quickness of discernment, their openness to religious impressions, their points of character... evidently qualify them ...for a more extensive field of usefulness.[15]

Finally, is it fair to rate Elizabeth as too mild-mannered to pass as a convincing militant? Unlike a suffragette in the twentieth century, admittedly, she did not chain herself in protest, even if there were plenty of leg irons for her to use. Elizabeth, indeed, hardly raised her voice. If she doesn't fit the usual idea of a pioneering feminist, it was more than just a matter of style. By being calm and rational at all times, Elizabeth wrung more concessions from the men in charge than noisy protestations ever would have done.

Despite Elizabeth Fry's contacts, her high social position, the support of her fellow Quakers, the greater participation of women in public life, it was little short of a miracle that she was allowed to initiate so many of her reforms at Newgate and elsewhere. As so often happens in England, the sheer chaos of the system facilitated the entry of a reformer. The burgeoning prison population existed largely because government and ruling class were at a loss to know how else to deal with problems, which they themselves had created. In the past law-breakers had usually either been executed, or pilloried and whipped. Even eighteenth-century society did not have the stomach to execute more than a few hundred people a year. Yet, the pillory and whipping were thought too lenient as punishments for offences, which were mainly against the sacred rights of property. Hence the use of prisons to breaking point, as continues today. Conditions in early nineteenth-century prisons were, however, unimaginably worse. Prisoners of all sorts – men, women, children, babies born in prison, murderers, lunatics, alcoholics, hardened and petty offenders, the untried, the innocent, were all herded together. Usually separate, though equally overcrowded, were the debtors, who numbered almost half the prison population. Disease was rife everywhere, because of the overcrowding, insanitary conditions, lack of clean water, absence of heating, light and fresh air, foul food, usually just bread boiled in water, and no straw to sleep on, except for those who could afford to purchase it themselves. Prisoners sometimes even lacked clothes. On entering the prison, gaolers would cry 'strip or pay!' – one of the many taxes they levied. The prisoner's only solace was cheap alcohol that the gaolers sold, as one of their many perks.

Given these appalling conditions, it may seem surprising that teams of well-bred ladies were allowed to see them. The main reason was that the prisons were farmed out to private individuals for profit. They were, therefore, not at that time, the direct responsibility of government, so until they became public property, some years later, there were no faceless bureaucrats to deny reformers entry. The Governor of Newgate, therefore, was as little interested in Elizabeth Fry's visits as he was unconcerned about the welfare of the prisoners themselves. The governor's attitude is well depicted in a later cartoon, in which he displays a gallant concern for Elizabeth's safety among those 'low savage creatures' while prudently refraining from accompanying her among them. It might be thought that the Governor would have been embarrassed that conditions in his prison should be revealed to the public. Yet, no one in his position needed to be concerned on that point, at least before Elizabeth Fry made her impact on elite opinion. Attitudes of the rich towards criminals and the destitute in general, were driven by fear. Although the power of the ruling classes was well entrenched, they seem to have been a prey to fears of insecurity. Fashionable London was terrorised by the mayhem of the Gordon Riots, which raged, for want of a police force, for several days on end. As Gibbon noted, 'the flames of London, which were kindled by a mischievous madman, admonished all thinking men of the danger of an appeal to the people'[16]. As for the French Revolution, that salutary example sent most of the reformers scurrying for cover – not just excitable poets such as Wordsworth, Southey and Coleridge, but even the leading Whig statesman, Charles James Fox. In short, criminals were seen as a threat to society, best hanged or transported to the colonies and otherwise left to rot in prison where they could remain out of sight and out of mind. Concern to uphold the law had very little to do with the imprisonment of the poor. Most serious crime – murder apart – was the speciality of the rich and powerful. The scale on which most of the leading politicians and aristocratic families plundered offices of state and exploited opportunities for patronage, make the depredations of the poor seem like innocence itself[17].

Elizabeth's work in Newgate is described so vividly by Dennis Bardens that only a brief word is needed here to set her achievement in the context of the long, and frequently interrupted, history of prison reform. Elizabeth wrought her 'miracle', as mentioned earlier, by accepting the female prisoners as human beings, in need of understanding and comfort. As she often pointed out, self-esteem was the key to moral regeneration. In any case, many of these so-called criminals, as she explained, were guilty of very minor offences, even if they might be hanged for them. It was society itself that had turned the poor to crime by its callous indifference to their basic needs. Elizabeth demonstrated in her work that treating people decently has such a tonic effect on their self-esteem, that it is the surest means of transforming their lives for the better. Many people seem to feel that the scriptural readings strike a false note of religious theatricality. It is easy to discount the reassurance, which many of the prisoners are likely to have felt, when they were told that there was a God, in whom many of them would have had some kind of belief, who actually cared for them. Just hearing Elizabeth reading aloud, whatever the subject, in her melodious voice, is likely to have had a calming effect. In any case, her approach was entirely practical. While Elizabeth's long-term aim was the salvation of souls, her immediate end was to bring material and psychological help. That Elizabeth and her helpers forged a bond, as fellow women with the prisoners served to boost their morale. For the majority of the female prisoners are likely to have been abused by men. It was probably for this reason that Elizabeth Fry placed so much stress on the separation of male and female prisoners. Though she was far too discreet to say it openly, she clearly suspected the gaolers and even the chaplains of raping the women. Hence her absolute insistence that women should care for women, quite apart from the fact that women might find it easier, as she believed, to confide in their own sex. A major reform was the introduction of a matron in charge of the prisoners. An extension of the idea was the choice of monitors, chosen by the women, from among themselves to help in the work of supervision. Behind these arrangements was the principle that all the rules for effective co-operation were with the full agreement of the prisoners themselves. This compact bears a striking resemblance to that between a therapist and a client today.

The practical measures prescribed by Elizabeth Fry all stemmed from her Quaker philosophy. She called for the 'classification' of prisoners, to separate the hardened criminals from the weak and minor offenders, so that the first should not contaminate the second. She started a little school for the children and wished to extend reading, writing and scriptural study to all. Knitting and sewing work, supervised by the monitors, provided a worthwhile occupation for the prisoners. As an incentive, a prison shop was established where the items made could be sold for the individual's benefit. Finally, Elizabeth established a few 'asylums' or refuges, where released prisoners could stay, while looking for work, to help prevent them from drifting back into crime.

The most eloquent testimony to the success of Elizabeth Fry's reforms at Newgate came from Sir Thomas Fowell Buxton, well known to the public for his leadership in abolishing the slave trade. In his influential *An Inquiry, whether crime and misery are produced or prevented by our present system of prison discipline* of 1818, he wrote:

It will naturally be asked, how and by what principles the reformation in Newgate is accomplished? How were a few ladies…enabled with such facility to guide those who had baffled all authority, and defied all the menaces of the law? …I found [when visiting Newgate] that the ladies ruled by the law of kindness, written in their hearts and displayed in their actions[18].

The success of Elizabeth Fry's methods had created so much public interest that a Commission of the House of Commons took the almost unthinkable step in that masculine chamber, of interviewing a member of the second sex. When she was asked to explain how she had managed to tame the female prisoners, who were likened popularly to wild beasts, Elizabeth replied simply: 'I think I may say we have full power amongst them, though we use nothing but kindness'. The Committee was so impressed, that she was urged to continue her work.[19]

Scarcely a quarter of a century later, the opinion of officialdom had swung totally against Elizabeth Fry's methods that had worked so well. The inspectors of Newgate in 1836 accused the ladies of going beyond their brief in directing the classification of prisoners and the appointment of female monitors. They were accused of introducing too many visitors. The prison shop, overseen by the ladies was singled out for condemnation, for being 'productive of much evil'. Meanwhile at the new prison at Millbank (built with slaving profits on the site of Tate Britain), the Rev. Daniel Nihill wrote an attack on Mrs Fry's methods and intentions. It is clear that he saw a ladies' association as a threat to his authority. Entry to the prison was sought, first through Buxton, then the Prime Minister, only to be refused.[20] If the work of Elizabeth Fry and her Quaker helpers had been singled out for attack, the reason might be attributed to personalities. On the contrary, official revulsion to caring superintendence in the prisons seems to have been universal. Alexander Maconochie, as Governor of the Norfolk Islands, of Australlia's east coast, in the 1840s, followed practices similar to those of Elizabeth Fry. He introduced a system of marks for good behaviour, honoured by early release, which reduced the reconviction rate. His political masters, unimpressed by his success, recalled him for being insufficiently punitive. Installed as Governor of Birmingham Prison, he used the same system, but was replaced by his sadistic deputy, who had the satisfaction of creating his own hell on earth.[21]

Most subversive of Elizabeth's reforms was fashionable support for the solitary confinement advocated by, among many others, John Howard and Jeremy Bentham. These ideas were first given architectural expression in the 'Gloucester Bastille' of 1792, followed in 1842 by Pentonville, which was to become a model for much of Europe.[22] Elizabeth roundly condemned both solitary confinement and its acolyte, 'the regime of silence'. 'Mrs. Fry's dread of the solitary system,' her memoirs record, 'was only augmented by further knowledge of its consequences. As permanent and a punishment for life, she considered it was too cruel to contemplate'.[23] Solitary confinement did, indeed, run counter to her policy of rehabilitating prisoners through loving concern and integration into a caring community. Officialdom in rejecting Elizabeth's methods had obviously failed to understand the secret of her success, or more probably had given way to their punitive instincts.

Why did it prove easier for Elizabeth Fry to reform the female prisoners in Newgate, than the authorities who ran the prisons? A feminist might be tempted to blame male chauvinism. Elizabeth Fry had certainly succeeded in making the male governor of Newgate and his fellows look very stupid. The governor had been too frightened to visit 'the savage women' on his own. Meanwhile a strange lady in quaint Quaker attire, armed with nothing more formidable than a Bible, soon had the female prisoners repentant on their knees. That was enough to make the first sex the laughing stock of the second!

Male exasperation, however understandable, is too simple an explanation for what amounted to a momentous reorientation in penal thinking. From the 1830s, a new 'scientific' penology was replacing the old. The notion of reforming criminals had come to seem old-fashioned. Solitary confinement and hard labour were now the fashionable prescriptions for remoulding lawbreakers to fit society's will; the more pointless and painful the work the better. Admirably suited to this purpose was the treadmill. Convicts at Cold Bath Fields Prison after six hours could achieve nothing more than climbing 8,640 feet. More punitive still was the crank, because it was worked alone without the company of fellow prisoners and the penalty for failing to execute the requisite number of turns was the loss of the next dose of prison gruel.[24] In breaking down the prisoner's resistance, preparatory to making him a law abiding Christian, solitary confinement was the tool par excellence, as described by a contemporary reformer, John Brewster:

> To be abstracted from a world where he has endeavoured to confound the order of society, to be buried in a solitude where he has no companion but reflection, no counsellor but thought, the offender will find the severest punishment he can receive...Left alone and feeling alive to the strings of remorse, he revolves on his present situation and connects it with that train of events which has banished him from society and placed him there.[25]

The overt intention of this punitive system was to destroy the convict's criminal character and to leave him with no alternative but to repent and assume gratefully the new persona given him by a morally responsible society. Banished, except in cases of non-co-operation, was corporal punishment, which had left society open to a charge of brutality. Henceforward, only the mind was to be tortured to the prisoner's benefit. These nineteenth-century English penal reformers surpassed the Holy Inquisition itself in casuistry.

The effects on the prisoners of solitary confinement and hard labour were to confound expectations. During the first eight years at

Pentonville, there were thought to be proportionately ten times more lunatics than in the population at large.[27] It may be assumed that most prisoners were too scarred by their experiences ever to resume a normal life.

As it was proved over and over again that the new punitive regime did not work, why didn't Elizabeth Fry's methods come back into favour? Michael Ignatieff in *A Just Measure of Pain: The Penitentiary in the Industrial Revolution, 1750-1850*, argues convincingly that the establishment had other ends in view, than the criminal's reformation. Prison reform was just part of a wider campaign to avert social disorder. The ruling classes during the early nineteenth century felt a prey to revolution. Besides the Gordon Riots and the French Revolution, there had been much sporadic unrest, leading up to the Reform Bill of 1832 and the Repeal of the Corn Laws in 1846, with the spectre of revolutions abroad in 1848. The ruling classes appear to have sensed that age-old paternalism no longer offered sufficient protection of their interests. In the eighteenth century a combination of *noblesse oblige* and some exemplary hangings, which also served to provide entertainment for the populace, appeared to work well as a means of social control. As the Industrial Revolution got under way, however, existing social structures came under pressure. Normally docile labourers, driven from the land by the enclosure movement, moved to the towns, where they became an underclass, outside authority's control. With an increase in population, came a rise in the number of paupers, who strained local resources. In response to what they saw as a widespread crisis in society, the governing class sought to tighten its control in two ways. The first was to recruit as allies the less well-off propertied classes by extending the vote to them. The second move was to contain the criminal and the poor, from whose ranks they came, in a network of institutions and regulations. The failure of the prisons to reform their inmates was immaterial. The function of the prisons was to frighten the poor into submission and to retain their more recalcitrant members out of sight and out of mind.[27]

When fears of revolution subsided, did incarceration decline and, where still necessary, become more humane? Readers hardly need reminding that they do not live in Utopia, but in twenty-first-century Britain.

The main reform in the later nineteenth century was the restriction of the death penalty to murder, treason, piracy and arson in Her Majesty's Dockyards. In the 1890s, there is some evidence of the revival of more humane attitudes. Charles Hopwood QC, liberal M.P., barrister and recorder of Liverpool, dared to reduce the average sentence of thirteen months and six days, before his appointment in 1886 to two months and 22 days by 1892, with a resulting significant reduction in crime. The Gladstone Committee at least attempted reform but were unable to reconcile their view that deterrence demanded severity, while harshness turned the prisoner into a hardened criminal. Although in the 1890s Colonel Sir Edward du Cane, Chairman of the Prison Commissioners, ensured that standards of severity were upheld, the Head of the Home Office presumed to toy with ideas of reform. He floated the notion that the crushing of self-respect, the absence of every opportunity to receive or give a kindness, the continual association with criminals, forced labour and the denial of all liberty are counter productive. Like a well-trained civil servant, he was quick to own that he had voiced a mere idea. 'In fact the unfavourable features I have mentioned are inseparable from prison life'.[28]

As for the twentieth century, a false dawn was followed by a dark night, which appears to be permanent. Winston Churchill, as Home Secretary for the Liberals in 1910-11, emerges as the most progressive holder of the office in the twentieth century. Churchill reduced the iniquitous prevalence of solitary confinement and urged greater use of probation. He even obtained a grant from the Treasury to provide concerts, lectures and books for the prisoners. Churchill's speech of 1910 would surely have pleased Elizabeth Fry: 'The mood and temper of the public in regard to the treatment of crime and criminals is one of the most unfailing tests of the civilisation of any country.' He urged 'the need for tireless efforts towards the discovering of the curative and regenerating processes, and an unfaltering faith that there is a treasure, if you can only find it, in the heart of every man.'[30] On visiting Pentonville, he was so shocked by the number of juveniles detained there for trivial offences, that he promptly released many of them, 'with a view to drawing public attention in a sharp and effective manner'. Churchill's wake-up call to consciences went unheeded. Home Secretaries imparted thereafter 'short sharp shocks' to juveniles, notably in the 1980s by Willie Whitelaw[30]. Around the time of the Second World War a mood of generosity swept through the country. Probation was extended and special Detention Centres to treat juveniles were created. A euphoric commentator even boasted that 'everything', Elizabeth 'asked of Parliament for her women in 1818 was granted by Parliament – in 1948'.[31] Considering the paucity of resources in post-war Britain, significant progress had been made.

The campaign for the abolition of the death penalty showed the precarious hold of liberal values upon the national conscience. The suspension of the death penalty for a trial five-year period in 1965 (which later became permanent) was secured in the teeth of the opposition of some 80 per cent of the population. The bill was only passed in Parliament after much political manoeuvring. Nor would it have taken place at all but for the eleventh hour Pauline conversion to Christian principles, which many bishops underwent in the House of Lords. That Episcopal lead played an essential role in swaying the votes of Tory MPs, who were reminded that 'the Church of England is the Conservative Party at prayer'. The bloodthirsty public's sense of *la trahison des clercs,* was given pungent expression by *The Daily Record.* The paper described Ramsey, the Archbishop of Canterbury, as expressing his pleasure at the passage of the bill, 'in a soft voice, as if trying to placate the ghosts of the nineteenth-century bishops, who would have burst their gaiters in horror'.[32] Elizabeth Fry had deplored the use of the death penalty nearly two hundred years earlier, on broadly the same grounds as the abolitionists. Progress had been made!

The following decades were to see a reversal of this progress. The most authoritative assessment of the situation today comes from the damning indictment in 1997 by Mr. Stephen Tumim, a recent Chief Inspector of Prisons:

> The outlook is gloomy, with policies encouraging over-crowding, and cutting of staffs and budgets, so that many inadequate people will be deprived of the education and psychiatric help they need. The gloom extends: a dying remand prisoner is shackled, a woman prisoner in labour is shackled in what seems to be inhumanity on a shocking scale.

Mr Tumim goes on to condemn 'the importation of "hulks" from America…These "hulks", prison boats anchored near the towns in the rivers or sea, were tried unsuccessfully as a means of holding prisoners in the eighteenth century and there is no reason to think them more feasible now.' The drug problem, he laments, goes unchecked to the point where new addicts are recruited in prison.[33] Elizabeth Fry would have been particularly concerned about the alarming increase in the number of women prisoners – 2.8% of all prisoners in 1990 and about 5% in 1999. The type of offences, coupled with the brevity of the sentences, show that most of these women present little risk to society, while the cost in suffering to the women and their families is often immense.[34]

In the appalling conditions within British prisons in the twenty-first century, it is understandable that so many prisoners have given up all hope, as the many suicides at Risley and elsewhere testify. Our period is unique in modern times, in that many of the reformers too have also lost hope. To quote Mr Tumim again: 'The true purpose,' is seen 'at vast expense to contain dangerous men and women where, for the time being, they could not commit more crime. This is the concept behind the modern phrase, "prison works". Are we justified in writing off a sizeable proportion of our younger population as uneducable and suitable for permanent exclusion from the community? Elizabeth Fry had asked similar questions in an earlier century when she wrote: 'Punishment is not revenge, but to lessen crime and reform the criminal." It may be that she says it all'.[35]

Those who are moved by Dennis Bardens' touching story of Elizabeth Fry, are unlikely to be happy with officialdom's complacent view that by removing criminals from society imprisonment works. Little is to be gained by direct appeal to either of the two leading parties. Their roll of oppressive Home Secretaries speaks for itself. Neither one is better than the other: it is pointless in Dr Johnson's words 'to distinguish between the precedence of a louse and a flea'. Nothing less than a sea change in public opinion will bring about change.

The public already has the instrument to bring about prison reform, if only they would support it. The Howard League for Penal Reform, which dates from 1860, has long been established as the foremost authority on the subject. Both a rallying flag for penal reformers and a sounding board for their views, the League provides them with the entrée to the establishment. Therein lies a classic moral dilemma. Reformers tend to see the authorities as enemy bastions that must be overpowered. That attitude smacks of the quixotic heroism of the Polish cavalry that charged against the invading German tanks in 1939. The Howard League has no legions behind it with which to threaten the authorities. Therefore, its best hope lies in co-operation – first to gain a sympathetic hearing, and then suggest reforms. The League has, indeed, achieved a great deal, especially considering the lack of interest in penal reform of almost all Home Secretaries, the tacit opposition of most of the legal profession, notably judges, of the police and many top civil servants. Relations with civil servants, however, are of crucial importance. Civil servants, better educated than many members of Parliament, are often more open to ideas. At the same time, civil servants tend to be too immersed in the arcane rites of their caste to have much contact with the outside world. The

Howard League is often a valued source of information on the practical running of prisons, about which civil servants are apt to know little. Civil servants fortunately need the League, as much as the League needs them.[36]

A reader of the *Howard Journal* is likely to be struck by the stark contrast between the excellent proposals for penal reform and the failure to put them into effect. Why is the public in general, especially the educated, so uninterested in the welfare of prisoners? Criminals, alongside immigrants, are doubtless useful scapegoats for a society, which still appears to be gripped by freestanding fear, which politicians and others habitually exacerbate for their own ends. The success of governments, since the nineteenth century in hiding prisoners out of sight, is surely an important cause of society's lack of concern. Whatever the reasons, a society with far greater resources, both in terms of money and psychological understanding, attempts proportionately less than Elizabeth Fry and a small band of Quaker assistants. Desperately needed is a pressure group among the public to give leverage to the Howard League for penal reform. Dennis Bardens will not have written in vain should he fire his readers to challenge the establishment and complete the work of Elizabeth Fry.

Dr John Mackrell, Queen Mary and Westfield College,
London University.

INTRODUCTION

Elizabeth Fry lived in harsh times. What would, to us, be evils were regarded then as natural and inevitable. The sufferings of the poor were taken for granted. Private duels, footpads, and highwaymen were common. The teeming slums of the big cities were dangerous territory into which few rich or well-dressed people dared to venture, except in groups, and then seldom after dark. Elizabeth Fry's willingness to go anywhere on a mission of mercy, confident that kindness would only be repaid with kindness, was an impressive act of faith and courage, the more so given that she was fearful as a child and had poor health.

Children at that period were not educated; even the children of the well-to-do went to boarding schools and public schools which were grim and over-crowded, where the food was often poor and scholarship encouraged by constant beatings and punishments. The textile trade, the main industry, was becoming mechanised so that people no longer carded and spun and weaved in their homes but had to go to large huts called factories where bad ventilation, over-crowding, dangerous working conditions and child labour were common. There were no police to protect life and property. Slavery still existed, and those who made fortunes from this human misery lived in respected opulence. Men were press-ganged into service with the Army and Navy, that is, simply seized on the streets and carried away often leaving their wives and children to starve. Discipline was maintained in the Services by cruel punishments and flogging. Not until 1850 did a law restrict this barbarous practice to fifty lashes and even that was often sufficient to kill a man. Nor was flogging restricted to men. Young children in the Navy sometimes no more than ten years old, were often 'encouraged' to climb the dizzy heights of the mast-head by a flourish of the villainous 'cat-o'-nine-tails'.

Children from the age of eight were employed as chimney-sweeps, forced to climb through the twisting, sooty labyrinth of strange chimneys, often choking with the soot, or becoming jammed; it was the practice to light straw underneath them to force them to wriggle out. Often they could not, and were suffocated. Sewers, in most parts of the country, were unknown, and even in big houses the sanitation was inadequate. Piped water supply was for most people an undreamed-of luxury. Crime was very prevalent, a result of the widespread poverty and temptation to steal, and the consequent punishments vicious. Public executions were considered public entertainments to which thousands of all ages, classes and sexes flocked together with hawkers, pie-men and pamphleteers, the latter selling the criminal's 'last confession' (almost invariably faked).

Between 1773 and 1800, the year Elizabeth Fry set out for London, the price of bread had risen five times and there had been ugly bread riots in Norwich and elsewhere. Shortly before she arrived, howling mobs had run amok in London, wrecking and looting homes, attacking anyone they found, setting fire to buildings and storming Newgate Prison, releasing the prisoners.

CHAPTER ONE

A Fearful Childhood

ELIZABETH GURNEY, as she was then, was born on 21st May, 1780, in a plain but roomy house in Magdalen Street, Norwich, in Norfolk, a picturesque market town with cobbled, winding streets, dominated by the fine old castle and cathedral. It was a period when men of means dressed richly and elegantly, travelled on horseback or in sedan chairs or by stage coach. George III was King.

Elizabeth's father, John Gurney, came of a distinguished Norfolk family descended from the Norman invaders; he was a banker and woollen manufacturer, and a member of the Quakers, or Society of Friends. Quakerism had arisen in the seventeenth century when England was in a ferment of religious ideas. George Fox taught that religion was a matter of first-hand experience, not of unquestioning acceptance of an infallible Church or an infallible Bible. "Christ saith this, and the Apostles say that, but what canst *thou* say?" he once asked. One of John Gurney's ancestors had been converted by the early Quaker preaching and the family had remained firm in his belief.

Elizabeth's mother, Catherine, also came of a distinguished family. She was a lovely, dark-haired woman with kind, expressive eyes and as a girl had been painted by Gainsborough. With a father who was young (thirty-one when Elizabeth was born), handsome, sociable and rich, a mother who was affectionate yet firm, beautiful and intelligent, she had a brother and two sisters to play with; Catherine was four years older, Rachel two years older, and John three years older. With such emotional support, some children would have been exceptionally happy. Elizabeth however was a fearful child and so terrified of the

1

dark that it was misery for her to be denied the comfort of a candle in the huge, gaunt room where she slept. The sea also frightened her, and when forced to bathe in it she could not conceal her terror: a recurrent nightmare for many years afterwards was to torment her of waves engulfing and drowning her. She frequently cried just because people looked at her. Often ill, she felt as though somebody had lifted her up by the heels and shaken all the energy out of her. Despite her nervousness and poor health, Elizabeth was entirely free from any bitterness, mean instincts, deceit, outbreaks of temper or dishonesty of any kind. She loved her father and mother, was devoted to her brothers and sisters, was always considerate and kind to the household servants. She did not, like some sick or unhappy people, blame others for her misfortunes, but always blamed herself. She believed in God as the source of all goodness and an inspiration to all His creatures to follow His example.

Elizabeth's father was not a 'plain' Quaker - one of those who adopted a sober mode of dress, and frowned on such pleasures as dancing and music. He liked fine clothes, having friends to breakfast, lunch or supper and giving concerts and dances at his home. However, he insisted that the entire family attend the weekly services at the Friends Meeting House. The children fidgeted miserably through the endless sermons. Every day Mrs. Gurney read to them a passage from the Bible.

Elizabeth spent the first six years of her life in this Norwich house, her companions apart from her immediate family being her governess and tutors, old Uncle Joseph, her father's brother and a strict Quaker but a lovable man; and the Gurney grandmother, who lived in a separate wing of the house. Although a rich woman, the old lady always gave away to the poor more than her entire income and depended on her children for support.

There was much to capture a child's imagination in the Norwich scene: the bustle and merriment of the twice-yearly fair, the busy market, the blare of military bands, the colourful costumes and dresses of the well-to-do, the men in buckled shoes, silk hose, velvet knee-breeches and patterned waistcoats; the women in elaborate dresses. But Elizabeth, a shy, sensitive child, was happier in her father's country cottage at Bramerton, with its garden full of flowers, its orchard heavy with summer fruit, the great oak and walnut trees and the dreamy River Yare winding through lush green meadows. In later years she compared it to Paradise.

Other brothers and sisters were born after Elizabeth, so that eventually she was one of twelve children. From the earliest age, the Gurney children were taught to talk to, and treat with respect and interest, the poorer country people. Her friends included a woman called one-armed Betty, and a kindly labourer called Greengrass, who grew the best strawberries in Norfolk.

The Gurney house was getting too small for his growing family, so in 1786 they all moved to Earlham Hall, a handsome, and historic mansion near Norwich, surrounded by old-world gardens and pleasant glades. There was room enough for everyone not only for the family, the servants and the many relatives, but also for Quaker friends who were always coming in for meals or staying for a few days.

Elizabeth's shy, timid ways and reserved nature made her withdraw from many of the pursuits of her more boisterous brothers and sisters. For them there were tree-climbing and horse-riding, gardening and rambling, besides music and singing songs together. In some of these Elizabeth joined, but often she felt ill. She rose in the morning later than the rest, and was often too tired to join in the dances which the Gurneys held from time to time.

Yet Elizabeth was greatly loved by her family. Her mother who, like most people of that age, kept a daily journal of her hopes, fears and activities, wrote of Elizabeth as 'my dove-like Betsy'.

The social life at Earlham was varied and interesting. Lessons were given by private tutors, and Elizabeth, as she later admitted, did not pay much attention to them. Rarely was she able to concentrate on her lessons and she never quite mastered the art of spelling. But she followed with interest the many discussions with guests and visitors, which included not only Quakers, but Anglicans, Roman Catholics and Free Churchmen - for Catherine Gurney did not believe in restricting her acquaintance to those of her own religious faith. She was content to give her children daily religious readings, to see that they attended Quaker meetings, to encourage them to pray, and to leave each to find his or her own individual path to goodness.

After centuries of religious strife - even the Quakers had been persecuted in their early days - England was enjoying a greater measure of religious freedom than ever before. There was a steady growth in the non-conformist churches - by which is meant those which did not conform to the prayer-book of the Church of England. Catherine Gurney believed that true faith could not be imposed by force.

The Gurney children, including Elizabeth, enjoyed the usual pranks and pleasures of a normal childhood. Once the seven sisters, wearing their scarlet cloaks, joined hands and stood boldly abreast in front of the Norwich stage-coach, forcing it to stop. Louisa, four years younger than Elizabeth (who was 'Betsy' to them all), was a merry, saucy little girl, always up to tricks and fond of dancing, singing and music. Rachel, her older sister, was the most beautiful. Catherine, the eldest girl, was mother to them all in Mrs. Gurney's absence. Sam was rebellious and always in trouble and was packed off to boarding school at the age of eight instead of at the usual age of twelve.

The 'plain' Quakers frowned on Betsy's scarlet cloak and purple soft leather boots with their red laces, which she actually wore at a Quaker meeting. They would shake their heads, too, when the blind fiddler arrived at the Gurney home and the girls enjoyed what they described in their diaries as 'a merry romp'. Both Mrs. and Mr. Gurney believed that pleasures were desirable in moderation, provided that they harmed no one and that in the course of enjoying them, they did not forget others less fortunate. The Gurneys had always given freely to charities, looked after their servants and employees and refused all chance of investment in dishonest or inhuman ventures. John Gurney, once invited to participate in a scheme called the 'Yarmouth Privateers', in effect no better than pirates, disowned any connection with them. That was enough to kill the plan.

The children did not greatly enjoy their weekly enforced pilgrimage to the Friends Meeting House in Goat's Lane, Norwich - a rather grim building in the Dutch style. Sometimes an eloquent preacher, perhaps a visitor from America or just some other county, would make Sunday interesting, but often the sermons were dull and long, and to Elizabeth's young eyes some of the older and stricter Quakers seemed very gloomy and severe. Along with the majority of her contemporaries, Elizabeth kept a private journal - over forty thick books, written in her own hand, exist today - in which the day's events and thoughts were recorded. Again and again, in her own and her sisters' diaries, occurs the significant entry 'Goats was *dis*' – the last a code word for 'disgusting'.

Often Elizabeth would join her sisters in singing. Indeed, years later, when she was seventeen, they sang for two hours to the Duke of Gloucester, nephew and later son-in-law of George III, who was stationed at Norwich with his regiment.

Elizabeth did not like having lessons and was especially poor at languages. Often, feeling drained of energy, she could not join in any games and was given to bouts of severe self-criticism and fear. Sometimes she was confined to bed for weeks on end.

In her solitude of sickness she often thought about religion. She could not make up her mind whether truly to believe or not. Many good people went to the Quaker meetings, while some visitors such as John Pitchford, a Roman Catholic, impressed her deeply with their quiet sincerity. Elizabeth wanted to be good, and wanted to believe, but although she succeeded in the first object, being loved by everybody in her family and outside, the second was not so easy.

When she was twelve years old, her mother died, only fifteen months after her thirteenth child (one had died) had been born. Her death was a terrible blow to Elizabeth, and in her grief she sought consolation in prayer. Catherine, the eldest, became mistress of the household and mother to the rest of the children, and Elizabeth, too, mothered some of the younger ones.

At the age of seventeen a crisis occurred in Elizabeth's life, a crisis which altered her whole attitude to the world. In February 1789 an American Quaker, William Savery, visited Norwich and preached at the Meeting House. She listened spellbound to his every word, and begged her Uncle Joseph to invite him to dinner so that she might meet him again and hear once more his reasons for his belief in God. She was so moved by the experience that she wept all the way home and recorded in her journal words which were to have a profound effect not only upon her life, but upon the lives of countless others she was to meet in later years. She wrote: "Today I felt that there is a God. I have longed for virtue. I hope to be truly virtuous."

CHAPTER TWO

Turning Point

At the age of seventeen Elizabeth Gurney was, her record of erratic health apart, a most attractive young woman. Her expression alternated between thoughtful repose and youthful gaiety and impudence. Her bearing was easy, her manner of dress tasteful. With her flaxen hair parted at the forehead and drawn up into a bun high at the back, her oval cheeks and fresh complexion, she looked very appealing in her white muslin dress, her poke bonnet, muff and cloak. The children mixed habitually with people who were able to afford to dress well, eat well, and employ servants. Like her brothers and sisters, Elizabeth was always neatly dressed.

To a great extent, Elizabeth, like all her family, had been sheltered from many of the realities of life. She had seen nothing of the world except Norfolk. Her personal friends were drawn almost exclusively from the educated classes and the well-to-do. She had been fortunate that both her mother and father had never cultivated friends simply because they had position and money. Both her parents had encouraged interest in music, literature and art. The friends and relatives who visited the Gurney household included evangelists, authors, landowners, musicians and artists, for her mother - now dead for five years - had had decided literary tastes.

Elizabeth, then, was far from being a gloomy girl. Although not so high-spirited as her sister Rachel, she nevertheless liked dressing up and dancing, animated conversation and social occasions.

Nor were her religious views very definite yet, despite the profound impression made upon her by hearing the eloquent William Savery.

Since her mother's death, and her elder sister Catherine becoming head of the household, the girls had enjoyed far more freedom than was customary in those days. Radical writers such as Voltaire, Rousseau and Tom Paine (who wrote an attack on religion called *The Age of Reason)* had all been read and discussed in the household. The Gurney children had learned to think for themselves, and shortly before hearing Savery, Elizabeth had written in her diary: "Today I have felt all my old irreligious feelings" - in other words, she was searching for a faith, something she could really believe and had not yet found it.

Her sisters were rather unhappy about Elizabeth's sudden seriousness, after that memorable meeting at Friends Meeting House. She began to dress more plainly, refused to join in their old pleasures of music and singing, boating and rambling and larking about, to such an extent that poor Rachel felt she was, in a sense, losing the playmate and friend she loved above all others.

Poor Rachel, writing her secret thoughts in her diary as usual, confided: "I felt extremely uncomfortable about Betsy's Quakerism, which I saw, to my sorrow, increasing every day. She no longer joined in our pleasant dances and singing . . . she dressed as plain as she could."

How pleasant some of those days at Earlham had been! A day in the lives of those girls, compared with that of most children in England of the eighteenth century, was pure pleasure. Imagine the day on which the young Catholic, John Pitchford, had come to spend the day with the Gurney girls. He came before six o'clock in the morning, soon after dawn had broken; the girls were up and dressed, calling greetings through the mansion windows as he came whistling up the drive. They read together in the shade of the gardens, enjoyed a sumptuous breakfast in the fine old dining-room, the table agleam with polished silver and the food served by servants. They went into the kitchen garden to pick fruit and eat it, settled by a haystack and read from each other's journals, then dressed for 'dinner' (which was at three o'clock), after which they played the piano and sang songs together. Then out in a boat, on the river Wensum, gliding through meadows and fields, laughing and joking in the summer sunshine. Tea in the garden, on to the village church to hear the singing, then a sing-song by the river's edge. They watched the sunset, and then back to Earlham for a merry supper.

In a world where poverty was rife, where there were no factory laws and women and young children worked long hours under disgraceful conditions, where flogging and hanging for the most trivial offences against the law were commonplace, where there was no compulsory education and most working people were illiterate, theirs was a pleasant world indeed. True, Elizabeth had always been taught to respect the poor and distressed and treat them kindly, but it was in her own nature to do so anyway; everyone remarked upon her gentle ways and tender consideration for other people.

Now she was searching her heart seriously, asking herself what she should do in life, how she should behave. Were the plain Quakers - those simple, honest people who turned their backs on pleasure to lead the good life - right after all? She wanted to test her beliefs in the wider world. To the surprise of her family, she asked to be allowed to spend some time in London.

It was a bold suggestion, but her father, who thought she was carrying things too far in giving up every innocent pleasure, hoped that the jolly atmosphere of London would cheer her up and restore her sense of proportion. He agreed. After all, Sam, her rebellious brother, was in London. John Gurney had many influential friends there, including John Opie, a distinguished artist who had been a frequent visitor to Earlham, and had painted a lovely picture of Rachel and Richenda having their fortunes told by a gipsy. The opera and dance, the busy streets of London with their shops and diverse people, would, he hoped, shake her out of her gloom.

And so, in a luxurious carriage owned by her father, protected from the March winds by cosy sheepskin rugs, Elizabeth Gurney set off with him for London, stopping for a night at an inn at Thetford. Her luggage contained many changes of dress suitable for elegant occasions. She had, in addition, numerous invitations from friends and letters of introduction from her father. He saw her comfortably installed in the mansion of his cousin Barclay, and returned to Earlham, leaving her to enjoy herself.

It was the London of the dandy, the over-dressed aristocrat who might wear a fortune on his back. It was a London of elegance, where fortunes were spent in a night in gambling at such clubs as Brook's and Boodle's. A glittering life revolved around the court but there was rebellion in Ireland and war with France, events which to Elizabeth seemed far, far away.

She threw herself into the social whirl, staying with one family friend after another. She went to Drury Lane and Covent Garden theatres, visited the opera, attended many a society dinner and ball. She enjoyed a stay with Mr. and Mrs. Opie, who were friends of Sir Joshua Reynolds, and through them met many people famous in the theatrical, musical, literary and artistic worlds. Yet somehow she felt she was pretending. There was pleasure to be had from these activities indeed, she thought, but they were not all of life; what of the brutalising slums she passed through? What of the horrifying public floggings and executions, which she did not see on this visit, but heard so much about?

It happened that the Quaker preacher, Elizabeth's personal hero, William Savery, was in London at the time, and was to address a meeting in Westminster. Elizabeth went to hear him, came once more under the spell of his piety and sincerity, and knew then and there that the comfort and pleasures which she had come to sample were not the things that mattered most to her. "May I never forget the impression William Savery has made on my mind," she wrote. "I thank God for having sent at least a glimmering of light through him into my heart.... May I never lose the little religion I now have... I feel there is a God and immortality."

She received a letter from him which strengthened her resolve to alter the course of her life. Her health had become poor again (she was, in fact, the victim of recurrent depression) and she was cheered by his words. It is not the sort of letter sent to people nowadays. It is almost like a sermon in writing, addressed to one person. But it was written with sincerity and shows that Savery had recognised in Elizabeth Gurney an exceptional person marked out for a special mission. "I know, my dear, thou hast and will have many temptations to combat with but it is very evident thou art under the especial care of an infinitely better Instructor, who has already uttered His soft and heavenly voice."

Deeply moved, and strengthened afresh in her resolve, Elizabeth returned home.

Back at Earlham, Elizabeth Gurney was completely changed. Her father and her sisters were disturbed and distressed, for she became almost fanatical in her adherence to strict Quaker principles. Dressing more plainly than ever, reading the Bible assiduously every day, listening intently to the ministry in the Quaker meetings for worship, which she once found so boring, and which her sisters found boring still, refusing to sing or dance or draw - it was, to the sisters, as though they had lost a companion. She even refused to look at a portrait of her father which the amiable John Opie was painting at the time.

Yet her new-found conviction was respected by her family, for there was nothing unfriendly or arrogant in her manner. She was more serious than ever, more determined and sure of herself and her ideas, yet ever polite, considerate and attentive. "Betsy," wrote her younger sister Richenda in her diary at the time, "seems to be changed from a complete sceptic to a person who has entire faith in a Supreme Being and a future state." Bob, a beloved servant, lay dying, and it was Betsy who with soft words and shining faith, could comfort his last moments with an assurance that death was not to be feared and that a protecting hand would guide him into immortality.

Elizabeth next decided on a clear statement of her aims and objects in life. They are very important, indeed, if we are to understand the rest of her life, because it was only by trying always to follow them that she was able to accomplish all her work:

First. Never lose any time; I do not think that lost which is spent in amusement or recreation, some time every day; but always to be in the habit of being employed.

Second. Never err the least in truth.

Third. Never say an ill thing of a person, when I can say a good thing of them; not only speak charitable but feel so.

Fourth. Never be irritable nor unkind to anybody.

Fifth. Never to indulge myself in luxuries that are not necessary.

Sixth. Do all things with consideration, and when my path to act right is most difficult, feel confidence in that Power that alone is able to assist me, and exert my own powers as far as they go.

The recurrent nightmares and constant fears which had plagued Elizabeth all her childhood now lifted. She still dreamed, as she used to, that the great waves of the sea were about to sweep over her, but the waters advanced only as far as her feet, and then receded. She was more assured in her approach to people. She no longer feared the dark.

John Gurney decided to take his family on a tour of England and Wales, stopping at inns or staying with Quaker friends at various places. In the course of this tour an old friend, Deborah Darby, who had long and earnest discussions with Elizabeth, made a remarkable prophecy; Elizabeth Gurney, she declared, would live to be "a light to the blind, speech to the dumb and feet to the lame". How could she know this? Nobody could explain it, but the old woman impressed the family with the certainty of her conviction.

The tour must have been a fascinating one. The family journeyed to Fareham, Dawlish, Plymouth, Abergavenny, Aberystwith, Caernarfon, Coalbrookdale. Everywhere they stayed with wealthy friends who owned large estates. It was a feast of changing scenery, exploring different homes and mansions, seeing historic places, attending dances and dinners. Often Elizabeth was 'much tired, quite fagged' and frequently she refused to join in the amusements. Taken to Plymouth Dock, and visiting a man-of-war, her thoughts were of the uselessness of war. "But after all the art, the expense and trouble, that men put themselves to, what do they gain, but the destruction of their fellow-creatures?" she asked. On the same grounds she refused to see a military review. By disposition she was opposed to war and militarism and as this was, and is, in line with the Quaker character. She felt strengthened more than ever in her determination to become a plain Quaker.

Back in Earlham, Elizabeth threw herself into social work. Walking in the park one day she saw a girl of her own age, a poor girl called Molly Norman, carrying a huge bag of flour. She looked so tired and shabby that Elizabeth felt ashamed of her own expensive clothes. What, she asked the girl, did her clothes cost a year? "Perhaps ten shillings - when we can afford it," the girl replied. Elizabeth saw her father, asked his permission to adopt Molly, pay for her clothing and keep, bring her to the house, and teach her some rudiments of education.

Soon she was 'adopting' others. The circles of her charges grew and grew, and became known to the family as 'Betsy's imps'. They came as a raggle-taggle army of neglected children with pinched faces and clothed in rags. She helped to clothe and feed them, read the Bible to them, gave them simple religious instruction and taught them to read and write. They would go on country walks, and she would explain the interesting features of the country's history, and identify wild flowers for them. By modern standards this may not seem much but at that time there was no public welfare state, no compulsory education. It was easy to starve or die when ill for want of medical attention. Elizabeth conducted her class at first in a huge eleven-sided attic in Earlham Hall, but later, as the numbers grew to seventy, an additional large room, that had been the laundry, was pressed into service.

It says much for the liberality and kindness of her father that he never in any way opposed this ministering to the poor, which was very unusual in those days. His family had, of course, always given generously to charities but had not until then taken any active part in the actual distribution of money and help. With Betsy, nothing was too much trouble. She would visit the sick and inquire from the people she met what was happening around her.

She was not seeking credit for herself. Her efforts to help were spontaneous. Living in Norwich, for example, was a poor widow of an army officer, who had married again and was expecting her first child. She had little money, no comforts of any kind and nobody to help her in her ordeal. One day the doorbell rang. It was Elizabeth, who had ridden on horseback from Earlham, bringing a basket of chicken and other delicacies. She simply left the basket and did not wait for thanks.

In the meantime, as she neared twenty years of age, her father thought seriously about marriage for her. He knew that she had been in love, at sixteen, with a ne'er-do-well called Lloyd, who had half captured her heart and then deserted her without a word. He was convinced that she had been half in love with the preacher William Savery; her sisters had told her bluntly that she was and although she had denied it her father noticed, when they attended his farewell meeting in the course of their tour, that Elizabeth had pressed a pocketbook into his hand as a farewell keepsake and seemed deeply affected by his departure.

It was high time, John Gurney thought, that his daughter should marry. With her impulsive nature, her great love of children and, on the other hand, her uncertain health, she needed someone to lean upon, somebody to provide a home for her so that she could make her own life. And with these thoughts in mind, it came about that he introduced her to a plain Quaker called Joseph Fry, who, like many others of his faith, came of a very wealthy family.

At the first meeting Elizabeth and Joseph got along very well together and he began to feature in her diary. He was honest, hard-working, friendly, cultivated, and particularly fond of music. In July 1799, he proposed to her, and was instantly refused. But he bided his time, and came again to Earlham in 1800, determined to try again. It was arranged that he should leave his watch and chain on a seat in the garden of Earlham. If she should pick it up, it would be a sign of her acceptance. While her sisters watched from behind the bushes, she approached the seat, looked at the watch and then turned and fled back to the house without touching it. The six sisters, however, did not go away. They thought she would come back again. And sure enough she did, this time picking it up. Although her marriage promised to be happy, yet leaving the home where she had spent fifteen years of her life, to part with her brothers and sisters and father, and perhaps most of all, to say good-bye to 'Betsy's imps' - now grown to a community of eighty-six - was a terrible wrench for her. She hugged and kissed every one of them individually, promised to follow their fortunes and keep in touch with them, and left as Mrs. Elizabeth Fry to live with her husband in London.

Elizabeth Fry set up Bible study lessons for women and children.
Courtesy of Mary Evans Picture Library

CHAPTER THREE

Life At Mildred's Court

Elizabeth Fry's journey to London in 1800 was long and arduous, with stops at different towns. On arrival, the great mansion in Mildred's Court looked inviting, with its sumptuous rooms, blazing fires, handsome furniture and silver, its liveried footmen and uniformed servants.

But it was in some disorder and Elizabeth was soon to discover how demanding being a wife and mistress of a large household could be. Some of the servants resented the new mistress and ignored some of her instructions. She hated stern measures, but it took time for her quiet firmness to be effective. Furthermore, her husband had a wide circle of business and Quaker friends who treated the household as their own. When the annual Quaker meeting was held in May, as many as sixty people would come and stay, and the superintendence of their rooms and the preparation of the huge meals were a great responsibility, for always food was prepared for some twenty or more people than the number who were expected.

Furthermore, many of her husband's friends were, by contrast to the Quakers she had known in Earlham, rather grim - opposed to the simplest pleasures, forever on the watch for 'sinful ostentation'. By comparison, her life at Earlham must have seemed like paradise indeed; she loved the countryside 'decorated', as she once put it, with wild flowers, and always went for a long holiday and reunion with her family every year.

There is no doubt that she found the busy city life a strain, but she would not give way to irritability, took an active part in Quaker worship and gave what time remained to social work.

Her visit in May 1801, to a Quaker educationist, Joseph Lancaster, who kept a school for poor children, began a friendship which was to last for many years, and to prove of great value. Lancaster had hit upon the idea of making one of the children a monitor, who saw that the children had their books, did their lessons and appeared for them at the right time. The 'Lancastrian method' led to schools on that pattern being started all over England over thirty years later.

Elizabeth's first child (she had twelve children) was born in 1801, and necessitated a long convalescence. Even the rich could not be spared the suffering of a difficult birth, for anaesthetics were unknown. But she loved the child, whom she named Catherine, after her own eldest sister, dearly and was a perfect mother.

France, which had been in the throes of revolution, had a brief respite with the Treaty of Amiens in 1802, and Elizabeth, sitting in the parlour of Mildred's Court above her husband's counting house, heard the clamour and noise of the London mob merrily celebrating it. "The noise of the mob," she wrote, "makes my head ache. It does not seem the right manner of showing our gratitude, as it appears to lead to drunkenness and vice."

Although constantly occupied with the cares of her increasing family, she nevertheless kept in close touch with her father, brothers and sisters, uncles and aunts, and also with a large and ever-growing circle of her Quaker friends. But none of these activities ever interrupted her continuing ministrations to the poor. She could write sorrowfully in her diary, constantly watching to see if she became selfish and worldly: "I am so continually devoted to the things of this world as to blind my spiritual sight." In fact, she never forgot the poor and the suffering. Often she visited the worst slums, simply inquiring for those in distress, and then doing something practical to help; perhaps sending her own doctor at her expense where there was sickness, or distributing food or clothes, or arranging for somebody's education.

On one occasion she was stopped, on a bitterly cold winter day, by a woman begging with a scantily-clad infant in her arms. Being a practical woman, and wanting to be sure that any help she gave would be used for the infant and not spent on drink, which she had known to happen many times, she asked the woman where she lived. The woman was evasive and made off but Elizabeth followed her to a dingy back street and up some rickety stairs into an incredibly filthy room where large numbers of children were lying ill and starving. Horrified, she returned home and sent her doctor along to tend them. But when the doctor arrived he found the squalid room empty and abandoned: the children had disappeared without trace.

Many deaths in the family, including that of her father-in-law, William Storrs Fry, whom she nursed zealously at Mildred's Court, had so worn down Elizabeth's health and wearied her that she wrote in her diary that after eight years of marriage she had become, instead of a militant church worker, 'a careworn wife and mother, outwardly nearly devoted to the things of this life.' Yet the very fact that she so persistently records these doubts shows clearly that she had not forsaken or dismissed from her mind her original ideal of being of real service in the world, and in doing what the God in whom she truly believed would desire her to do.

Her greatest grief was, undoubtedly, the death of her father, John Gurney, at Earlham in 1809. Although ill herself, she made the long and difficult journey to Norfolk by stage-coach, arriving just before he died. The funeral was at the beautiful old Gildencroft meeting house in Norwich, and at the graveside she fell upon her knees and offered a prayer, not of grief, but of thanks for the happiness they had known together and the eternal happiness which, she implicitly believed, awaited him. It was, as she afterwards recognised, a turning point in her life. All doubts that there might not be a God were finally dispelled. Believing in a Divine Will, she was sustained by her faith at a time when grief might have broken her.

The death of her husband's father, William Storrs Fry, meant that they inherited his estate and home at Plashet, a hamlet near East Ham, and that, to her great joy, they could now enjoy a country home and sometimes escape from the noise and bustle of London. Not that she disliked London altogether. She was, until the end of her life, intensely interested in people. She was not a reformer who thought in terms of theories and schemes first and then applied them. Her first reaction on meeting anyone was always: Who are they? What do they do? How do they earn a living? Where do they live? What are their problems? What can I do to help? She did not accept poverty and suffering as an inevitable part of the ordinary scheme of things, as so many of her rich friends did.

Apart from her own individual acts of practical kindness, which are too numerous to list, she had in 1806 been appointed by the Friends of Gracechurch Street a visitor to the Quaker school and workhouse in Islington. She would read to them from the Bible, distribute religious tracts, help to organise their games, teach them to keep themselves neat and clean, and provide them with essential clothes. Her personality was an unusual mixture of extreme mildness and firmness. Children instantly liked her and they also obeyed her from an instinctive feeling that she was a good person, always reasonable in her demands.

Immediately she moved into Plashet, Elizabeth Fry bestirred herself on behalf of the poor in the district. Opposite the gate of Plashet House was a dilapidated dwelling, large and picturesque but starved of paint and attention. It was inhabited by an aged couple, brother and sister. The sister was an invalid, and although they had once known better days, they now eked out a living by selling rabbits.

The old lady sat, day after day, propped up in cushions, in an easy chair by the old Dutch tiled fireplace, bravely resigned to her approaching end. She was a kindly, refined woman, but disinclined to speak freely or make contact with people. Being proud, she feared that she might be thought to complain if she talked frankly of her circumstances, for she could hardly do so without inviting pity.

Tactfully, Elizabeth Fry spoke to her of the poor children of the neighbourhood, and how it lay in the couple's power to make their lives happier and more useful. The house would make an ideal school, for its large rooms were mostly unused. She talked of her friend Lancaster, and his success with children who once had been wholly illiterate and ignorant of decent living. So, under the influence of Elizabeth's persuasive eloquence and obvious sincerity, the old lady agreed to the largest room being used for a schoolroom. It was an excellent arrangement: the rent helped the old couple, and the school helped the poor.

Elizabeth became a familiar figure, too, at 'Irish Row', a wilderness of filthy hovels, near Plashet, which all too inadequately housed a poor Irish colony of labourers. Once she appeared in the depths of winter, when she herself was ill, laden with blankets to keep them warm. When a poor labourer died, she was there to comfort the family and relieve their distress. She loved these wild, warm-hearted people and they loved her. There was something sad and yet impressive in their desire to show their respect and affection, greeting her, clamouring round her, beseeching her to "come in here, Madame Fry", and "do step in here". Her selflessness, for one of her class, was something they were not used to. Their respect showed in small but telling ways, as when, Molly Malone, in rags with her dark hair dishevelled, insisted on Elizabeth having the only seat she could proffer, an upturned bucket, tenderly dusted with her apron, while the startled chickens, which shared the single room, fluttered and screamed from the potato heap in the corner. The Roman Catholic priests, who frequently visited the colony, warmly welcomed her attentions despite their religious differences.

There was also a gipsy encampment in Green Lane, about the time of Fairlop Oak Fair. These tough, swarthy, clannish people, who spoke their own distinctive language of Patteran and observed their own customs, accepted her as a friend at once, although by nature insular, from long experience of persecution. Sometimes, when she saw a sick child not receiving the attention it should, she would hold it in her lap, speak soothingly to it and give the mother simple medical advice. Often she would, with the parents' permission, vaccinate the children herself having learned the simple operation from her friend Dr. Willan, an ardent advocate. As a result, the dreaded disease of small-pox was unknown in Plashet.

These various activities of hers had not gone unnoticed in Quaker circles. Although it is true that some of the Quakers were, by modern standards, rather forbidding people who frowned upon the most innocent pleasures and seemed to take life far too solemnly, they proved a useful social influence by emphasising that religion does not consist solely in following whatever faith happens to be fashionable, or acceptable to the prevailing government, nor does it consist merely in conformity to ritual and regular attendance at a place of worship. These, they taught, were but outward signs of belief and unless trans-lated into action were meaningless. By their own way of living, they tried to demonstrate that everyone has some measure of responsibility for the happiness and welfare of their fellow-men, instead of lives pursued for purely personal and selfish ends.

When the Quakers meet for worship they do not have any specially appointed priest or minister to conduct the service. They sit down to worship God in silence believing that he may use anyone present to minister to the needs of the others. William Savery on that famous Sunday in February 1798 was given words which touched the heart of young Betsy, and she had herself been moved to offer a prayer at her father's graveside. Since then she had felt called upon from time to time to 'appear in the ministry' (as the Quakers say) and in 1811 she was acknowledged as a minister, which meant that her fellow-members believed she had a special gift in this direction which they were encouraging her to use.

By now she had seven children of her own to rear - four girls and three boys - so that, with the responsibility of running a school, her relief of the poor, her constant attendance at Quaker meetings and her warm and extensive hospitality, there was little likelihood of her slipping into the habit of laziness, against which she was constantly on guard. Yet, she was already on the brink of her new way of life.

CHAPTER FOUR

Newgate Prison

One of the landmarks of eighteenth and nineteenth century London was Newgate Prison. Architecturally, it seemed to the outsider very imposing. One contemporary writer described it as 'a marvel of strength and solidity'. Another, Hepworth Dixon, wrote that 'Of all the London prisons, except the Tower, it alone has an imposing aspect. The solid masses of its granite walls, strong enough to resist artillery, unbroken by door or casement - save those low and narrow slits in the centre, iron-bound and mounted as they are - frown down upon the great arteries of London.'

Inside it was dark, evil-smelling, over-crowded, and sinister; and although only recently rebuilt still carried on the inhuman tradition of a penal system based on spite, vengeance and cruelty. Prison was a punishment and there was no limit to what society was prepared to do to those who broke its laws.

Newgate had earned a dismal reputation ever since the fourteenth century, when it was also the scene of much misery, injustice and degradation. Even in 1334 an official inquiry stated that: "Prisoners detained on minor charges were cast into deep dungeons and there associated with the worst criminals. All were alike threatened, many tortured, till they yielded to the keeper's extortions, or consented to... swear away the lives of innocent men. These poor prisoners were dependent upon the charity and good will of the benevolent for food and raiment."

In 1381, the prison had been almost demolished by Wat Tyler's followers during his rebellion. In 1414, so foul were the conditions that the keeper and sixty-four of the prisoners died of plague. Here, in 1535, eleven monks who refused to acknowledge King Henry VIII as head of the Church, were incarcerated, being chained upright in a dungeon, where ten of them died from filth and disease, while the other was executed. Here, in 1670, Claude Duval, the infamous highwayman, was a prisoner. So, too (from 1702-3) was Daniel Defoe for writing *The Shortest Way with Dissenters*. Famous prisoners about to be executed were exhibited to the public for a shilling a time in Elizabeth Fry's day. In fact, going to see the 'Execution Service' was a favourite amusement with Londoners.

In 1780, the year of Elizabeth Fry's birth, 'No Popery' rioters had wrecked the prison, forcing open the great gates with crowbars, tearing away the roof and rafters, and releasing from the noisome dungeons twelve women and eight men, heavily laden with chains. Rebuilt, the new prison was completed in 1783: reputedly a model of its kind, but to the prisoners immured there a fearsome place.

In 1777, John Howard, a Fellow of the Royal Society, had published a voluminous report on the state of Britain's prisons, in which, with telling detail collected with immense labour and, on occasions, no little risk, he listed the enormities of the existing prison system. The prisons were intended to keep people in safe custody; little else was considered. People went in healthy, and in a short time succumbed to disease, for there was insufficient heat and warmth, no bedding in the bitterest winter, and scarcely any food. The sanitary arrangements were primitive, inadequate or even non-existent.

Howard found that in half of the prisons, debtors had no bread "although it is granted to the highwayman". Lingering on 'water-soup' (a little bread boiled in a lot of ordinary water) one debtor remarked: "We are locked up and almost starved to death." Often the keeper of the prison pocketed the allowance for food - which was meagre enough, varying from three to twelve ounces of bread a day - for himself, leaving his charges to starve. Cells usually had little air and the incidence of window-tax further reduced the number of windows.

A debtor might find himself incarcerated for twenty years or more through inability to pay some small debt and there could be no hope of his paying it since he had no means of earning money. Even small children would be bound in chains. Petty offenders, hardened murderers, and even dangerous lunatics whose shrieks and groans were enough to drive them insane, were all thrown together.

'Garnish' - the iniquitous custom of demanding from each new prisoner, on arrival, a sum of money for the gaolers, was often tantamount to a death sentence on those who had no money. "Pay or strip" was the cruel demand, and the wretched prisoner would have to forfeit part of his or her clothing. Denied even straw to sleep on, prisoners would, almost inevitably, catch pneumonia, or chills, or rheumatism or skin diseases caused by the chafing of flesh against the bare boards and stones. Many of the prisoners were loaded with heavy irons which ate into their ankles and wrists causing gangrene. Drink was sold to those who could afford it, to provide profit for the gaolers, and fights, assaults and drunken brawls were common.

Howard's report aroused the conscience of many reformers, but the evils to which he drew attention still flourished in Elizabeth Fry's time; it was so easy for these prisoners to linger on in misery, and for the outside world to be uninterested or ignorant of what happened behind closed walls.

Newgate Prison, which was to attract Elizabeth's attention, had figured in Howard's report. It was, of course, always a byword for suffering, but Londoners hardened by such revolting spectacles as public hangings and floggings often actually revelled in the sufferings of its inmates. The farce of the 'execution service', when the condemned were forced to sit in a special pew, exposed to the gaze of a curious public who had paid a shilling to watch them, was itself a mockery of religion. The condemned pew contained, as if to torment prisoners with thoughts of what lay ahead, a coffin. The parson would drone on about sin and its inevitable punishment, while the condemned had no choice but to listen. Small wonder that Richard

Carlile, a political prisoner at Newgate, commented after his release: "Christianity appears more hateful to me every time I reflect on this circumstance." But there were a few Christians who not only believed in and accepted implicitly the Christian doctrine of mercy and forgiveness, but translated their beliefs into action. Elizabeth Fry was one of them.

In 1811, Elizabeth Fry was drawn more and more into social and philanthropic activities, although the strain of raising such a large family - her eighth child "a swet little girl" (Mrs. Fry could never spell) was born on 12th September 1812, necessarily took up most of her time. Yet, despite her erratic health, she was an extraordinarily energetic person. This was just as well. She needed to be, in order to rear eight children, and there were more to come, to run her school at Plashet, to visit the poor, attend Quaker meetings, entertain Quaker personalities, encourage and attend meetings of the Norwich Bible Society, nurse or visit various relations when they were sick or bereaved, counsel and help her eleven brothers and sisters, manage the servants of two houses and assist in the management of her husband's estates. This kept her on the go almost sixteen hours a day.

Time, she firmly believed, was meant to be usefully employed, and when her husband seemed inclined to be easy-going, and liked to lie in bed late in the morning before going to his office, she set an example by getting up as early as four o'clock and seeing to the affairs of the house.

In 1813, just after Napoleon's invasion of Russia, and his disastrous retreat from Moscow in the depths of a bitter winter, which cost him nearly all his vast army - sad stories began to reach Elizabeth Fry's ears about the state of affairs in Newgate Prison. One of her informants was an American Quaker of French extraction, Stephen Grellet, who had called a meeting with the help of London Quakers of London's underworld, an alarming congregation of thieves, street-walkers, drunkards and pickpockets. The service was held in the Quaker Meeting House in St. Martin's Lane and Grellet was touched to the heart to observe how they responded to kindly concern. To a Christian, he maintained, nobody was 'lost'.

Continuing his work, Grellet decided to visit a few prisons, including the infamous Newgate. The prison authorities warned him against so foolhardy a venture; he would be set upon by the prisoners and robbed, and his clothes torn from him. Brushing aside their warnings, he had gone, and seen for himself the almost incredible misery there. In the bitter winter, he found people lying sick and frozen on bare boards, and "there were several children born in the prison among them, almost naked". Grellet saw these children - dirty, under-nourished, unclothed and unwanted by all except their mothers - as a ruthless vengeance by society upon the innocent. Aghast, he called on his friend Elizabeth Fry, and told her in graphic terms what he had seen. So, too, did another friend, William Forster, who had visited four people condemned to death in January 1813, and who in gaunt and solitary cells, awaited their painful and humiliating ordeal - all the mockery of being exhibited for money first and then finally executed in public. The stone walls were so thick that no sound could penetrate within or without; the thin slit of a double-grated window admitted scarcely any light or air; the walls were lined with thick wooden planks studded with heavy nails, and the vaulted roof reached a height of about nine feet. They were as near tombs for the living as inhumanity could make them. John Howard, in his report on prisons, said "criminals who had affected an air of boldness during their trial were struck with horror, and shed tears, when brought to these darksome solitary abodes."

Elizabeth Fry's first thought, however, was for the children. She loved children and understood them; she was also an intensely practical person. Accompanied only by a close friend and Quaker, Anna Buxton, a sister of Sir T. F. Buxton, her brother-in-law, she made her way to Newgate in a post-chaise, heavily laden with warm clothing. The military guards outside the gates allowed her to pass inside, but the Governor was horrified at her suggestion that she be allowed to visit the female prisoners.

"Madam," he said, solemnly but politely, "your clothes will arouse their envy and greed, and they will almost certainly tear them from you. They are completely lost to all decency; they are lewd, drunken, blasphemous, dirty, dishonest and violent."

"I will observe for myself what manner of women they are," replied Mrs. Fry, quietly, "but for the moment I am concerned with their conditions."

"This is a prison, Ma'am, a place of punishment. They're criminals, and they're treated like criminals."

"But are they all equally criminal? Some, I believe, have committed murder, but others are there for stealing objects of trifling value, worth a few shillings? Should they all be treated alike?"

"I don't make the law, Ma'am. True, some are bad criminals and others less bad, but we can't have a separate prison for each kind, can we? We've only got one quadrangle for them, so they're all in together."

"But the children," persisted Mrs. Fry, "is it fair to punish them, too? They have committed no offence, those born in the prison, I mean?"

"No, Ma'am, though I doubt if any children born of women like them could ever be any good to anyone. But where else would we put them? We can't turn them outside into the snow. Well, I can see you're determined to go inside; I can do no more than warn you, but I will not oppose your visit, for I know your intentions are of the best. But I implore you to leave your watch behind - they'll steal it."

"I am not afraid," was her reply. "Please take me to them."

The little party made its way through the dismal stone corridors. They were damp, cold and lit only by the fitful glare of a few gas brackets. An appalling smell filled the air and became worse as they got further inside; so close, foetid and objectionable that Elizabeth had difficulty in breathing. At last they reached the heavy iron gates of the women's quarter. This consisted of two wards and two cells, separated from the main quadrangle, where the male prisoners lived, by a wall over which they could look easily. Newgate had accommodation for only sixty females, yet at the time of Elizabeth Fry's visit, over three hundred were crammed into this space.

The noise and pandemonium were deafening. But the sight was terrifying, so much so that even the Governor never ventured inside. In this confined space three hundred women lived, slept, ate, washed. There was no bedding, except for a few lucky ones who had been able to bring, or beg, enough money to buy a little dirty straw. Most of the women were in rags. Some were emaciated with starvation, others wild and hollow-eyed with misery and fear, others drunk with spirits which they had bought in the prison, and were dancing and yelling curses at anyone and everyone. Some of the tiny children cowered terrified in a corner; other children, completely out of control, tried to outdo their elders in rowdyism. Most of the women looked more like wild beasts than human beings.

Although the turnkey feared for Mrs. Fry's safety, he unlocked the gate and let her in, alone, among them. To his amazement, he saw the company become quiet and look with incredulity at the lady of refinement who dared to risk coming into their midst. Her gentle bearing, quiet manner and utter humility made their mark upon them, and her tender way with the distressed children moved some of them to tears. She and her friend moved swiftly from child to child, distributing clothing, ordering straw as bedding from the warders, tending to the sick, speaking comforting words to the mothers. Instinctively the women, despite their depravity and coarseness, recognised in Elizabeth Fry an exceptional woman of outstanding integrity, someone who really cared for them and did not despise them or mock them in their misfortune. It was a unique experience for them. The dismal meanderings of the official clergyman at the endless Sunday services often aroused in them nothing but contempt; her quiet words reawakened their belief in God. "You are all God's children," she said, "and whatever trials you have to bear, He will never forsake you." Before they left, Mrs. Buxton said a prayer. Mrs.

Fry followed, and suddenly, as if by some secret signal, the wretched prisoners went on their knees and listened in silence. Some wept openly.

Mrs. Fry made several such visits, and records in her diary: "Yesterday we were some hours at Newgate with the poor female felons. It was a striking scene, the poor people on their knees around us, in their deplorable condition."

And writing to her sons, then staying at Earlham, she said: "I have lately been twice to Newgate prison to see the poor prisoners, who had little infants almost without clothing. If you saw how small a piece of bread they had every day, you would be very sorry, for they have nothing else to eat, unless their friends give them a trifle..."

Elizabeth Fry's new sense of mission needed, for the moment, more time than she could spare without neglecting her many other obligations, especially towards her family. In the business slump which struck England then - due largely to the war with France, culminating with the defeat of Napoleon by Wellington at Waterloo - Mr. Fry's business was badly hit, and economies were necessary. Her two oldest girls were sent to stay with their aunt, Rachel and her brother Daniel. The two older boys went to boarding school. Two others, Richenda and Joseph, were sent to stay with her brother Sam and his wife. Little Elizabeth, born in 1811, had died at the age of five. Mrs. Fry was left for the moment only with her youngest child, Hannah.

This may seem strange in modern eyes, and some have accused her of farming out her children in order to secure greater freedom for herself. This was not so. Her purpose was to effect an economy without making any noticeable change in their manner of living, and thus maintaining her husband's standing in the business world. Obvious cutting-back would only have tended to reduce the family's fortunes even further. Elizabeth's brother and sister were only too pleased to have the upbringing of the children and could afford it. Her own journals show that she missed her children sorely, and felt she parted with them for their own good.

Although, in the next four years, Elizabeth continued to visit the poor, she was largely absorbed by family affairs. The memory of Newgate still haunted her, but not until 1817 did she devote more time to the awful state of Britain's prisons.

CHAPTER FIVE

Hell Above Ground

I n the bitter winter of 1816-17, Elizabeth Fry began, in real earnest, to attempt some improvement in the pitiable conditions in Newgate Prison, which a writer of the period (who once went to see Mrs. Fry at work) described as 'hell above ground'.

John Howard, the prison reformer who had died when Elizabeth was ten years old, had confined himself, in his masterly survey, *The State of the Prisons,* to the prevailing conditions. It is true that his exposure of these shocking conditions, the injustice and the abuses had attracted much notice, and that tardy orders had been issued for some of the ranker abuses to be stopped. But nobody enforced the order or in any way exerted supervision, and the jail governors, warders and turnkeys ran things as they pleased. The old evils of 'garnish' over-crowding, lack of sanitation, drunkenness and brawling, continued unabated.

Mrs. Fry as a practical woman, focused her attention less on conditions prevalent in the prisons, than on the plight of particular women and children. Her tender heart was incapable of the common hardness and indifference to the spectacle of human suffering so general in her day: to most people a woman awaiting execution in Newgate was nothing more than a name in the newspaper or the butt of some coarse joke, but to Elizabeth Fry she was a human being, a woman whose tears and remorse, terror and loneliness touched her heart as much as if the woman had been her own sister.

She had seen for herself the terrible plight of the children in Newgate, both those who were juvenile delinquents and those who had simply the misfortune to be born in prison, and so remained there. She had seen children as young as seven years laden with chains, others half naked and shivering with cold, others drunk with the spirits which their drunken parents had bought in prison.

She had observed a good deal, but there was much more yet to see. Thomas Fowell Buxton, who besides trying to reform young criminals, campaigned actively for the abolition of slavery, wrote at this time how he had been distressed, on a visit to Newgate, by "the boys, forty-four little wretches, some of them under sentence of death." Although the death sentence on children was now commuted, the dismal ritual of condemning the children was still enacted in full, and being ignorant of the law and mostly illiterate, they suffered long agonies of mental torture. In any case, the conditions in which they were imprisoned were a sort of living death.

Elizabeth Fry had taken the initiative in forming The Society for the Reformation of Prison Discipline. It included her brothers-in-law, Samuel Hoare and Fowell Buxton, a Mr. Peter Bedford, William Crawford, Dr. Lushington, the Hon. E. Harbord, and several others. Her own position, as the wife of a prominent banker and businessman, and a leading Quaker, gave her access to people of influence, and secured her the necessary permission to visit Newgate whenever she pleased. A person of lesser social status would certainly never have got the hearing she did; but one must also remember that she herself had a calm yet persuasive personality which impressed everyone she met.

Visiting Newgate in the winter of 1817, her first main concern was the children. They were pining for want of fresh air, food and exercise and growing up degraded, undisciplined and illiterate. On her second visit, Mrs. Fry asked to be left alone with the women in the quadrangle. Her quiet manner, plain Quaker costume and obvious sincerity quietened the shouting mob. "Do we want these poor children to grow up into criminals?" she asked them. "They are *our* charge and our responsibility. Is this the best we can do for them?" She asked if they would co-operate if she started a school for the children within the prison. They would be taught decent ways, and would learn to read and write, and be given instruction in the Scriptures. She won the day. The women were deeply moved. There was absolute silence as she concluded her visit by reading to them, from the twentieth chapter of St. Matthew, the parable of the vineyard.

Elizabeth Fry obtained, without difficulty, the enthusiastic consent of the prison governor and the Sheriffs of London. They did not entertain a great deal of hope for the project, but they had observed what remarkable influence she had with unruly prisoners.

She appropriated a disused cell, had it whitewashed, and with a friend, Mary Anderson, and other helpers, started a school for twenty-five children. With pathetic care, their mothers struggled to send them in neat and clean. The saddest thing was the anxiety of the women themselves to be allowed to join in the classes, but there was simply no room for them.

A young prisoner, Mary Connor, was chosen by her fellow-prisoners to act as mistress. She was a quiet, well-behaved woman, who maintained firmly that she was innocent of any crime. She may well have been, for fifteen months later she was granted a free pardon. It was too late, however, for her to re-establish herself in life since she had contracted tuberculosis in the foul air of Newgate and shortly died of it.

The school, which did something to bring a whiff of decent civilized behaviour into Newgate, was an instant success. But we must not underestimate the courage and patience required to attempt work in such conditions. Mary Anderson, less accustomed than Mrs. Fry to the miseries of Newgate, described her visit there to start the school:

"The Railing was crowded with half-naked women, struggling together for the front situations, with the most boisterous violence and begging with the utmost vociferation. She felt as if she were going into a den of wild beasts, and she well recollects quite shuddering when the door closed upon her...."

Another helper, Elizabeth Pryor, comments how, "in our visits to the school …we were witnesses to the dreadful proceedings …on the female side of the prison; the begging, swearing, gaming, fighting, singing, dancing, dressing up in men's clothes; the scenes are too bad to be described."

She also saw one prisoner 'yelling like a wild beast', rushing round the prison with upraised arm, tearing the hats (linen caps) from the head of any woman in her path. This same person, by the way, later yielded to the religious teaching of Elizabeth Fry, and on leaving prison married and became 'a well-conducted person'.

Elizabeth Fry realized that in grappling with the general and widespread cruelty of her period, one thing at a time was a good motto. She could not hope to effect improvement everywhere at once. But having done something, at least, for the children at Newgate, she thought of the women, visiting them and gaining a terrible insight into nineteenth-century inhumanity.

Although women in Elizabeth Fry's time were dubbed the weaker sex and in principle spared exposure to risks and hardships, they were in reality treated with unutterable cruelty. Sentences of death were passed quite freely upon them, and they were also subject to cruel floggings, long prison sentences and transportation to one or other of the colonies for life. Often death sentences were passed on women on the flimsiest evidence or for simply being associated with somebody who had been convicted of an offence, and considered, therefore, an accessory after the fact.

Executions at Newgate were not something remote or private. They took place outside the door of the Debtor's section of the prison, with the Sheriffs and other officials in attendance, the bell tolling mournfully, and with the public watching. Prisoners awaiting execution on another day heard these proceedings, and were reminded constantly of the fate that awaited them.

Elizabeth Fry always visited women in Newgate awaiting execution, and saw for herself how intense were their sufferings, humiliation and agony of mind.

A particularly sad case was that of Elizabeth Fricker, sentenced to death in 1817 for being an accessory to the robbing of a house. On 4th March Mrs. Fry visited her in the condemned cell, to find her 'hurried, distressed and tormented in mind. Her hands cold, and covered with something like the perspiration preceding death, and in a universal tremor. However, after a serious time with her, her troubled soul became calmed.'

Poor Elizabeth Fricker! Indeed, her soul might be troubled, for she was confined in this noisome, clamorous, dismal place awaiting a death she had done nothing to deserve. She was filled both with terror, and a burning sense of injustice. It was claimed at the trial that she had let the burglar, Kelly, into the house. In fact, a day before he was to be executed, Kelly sent for the chaplain, Mr. Cotton, and maintained that Elizabeth Fricker was innocent, and that he had been let into the house by a young boy concealed there for the purpose. Dr. Cotton implored Kelly, a hardened rogue entirely without conscience, to make a formal confession and reveal the name of his assistant, and not allow an innocent woman to go to the scaffold to save an accomplice. Kelly refused to do this without a definite promise of pardon for himself. Although the authorities were informed of this situation, and desperate efforts were made to save her, Elizabeth Fricker was executed.

Then there was poor Mrs. Woodman, mother of seven children and due to have another. Although in this condition, she was condemned to death with her husband, and only allowed to live long enough to give birth to the child. She was executed a week later. Her husband, on hearing that she had been condemned, and wild with grief at the thought of her death and of the eight little children being left orphans, completely lost his reason, and had to be restrained in a strait-jacket. Mrs. Fry, on this visit, saw the turnkey come out of the cell, hugging a bleeding hand, which the poor crazed creature had bitten. One visitor paints a harrowing picture of Mrs. Woodman, lying lonely and terrified after the confinement in her prison cell: "She seems afraid to love the baby, and the very health which is being restored to her produces irritation of mind."

Perhaps an even sadder case was that of Harriet Skelton, whom Mrs. Fry tried so hard to save. She was convinced of her innocence, and wrote of her: "A very child might have read her countenance, open, confiding, expressing strong feeling, but neither hardened in depravity or capable of cunning. Under the influence of the man she loved, she had passed forged notes."

Harriet's act seemed hardly deserving of death. She had done what the man she loved told her to do. She could even have saved her life had she known more of the law, which she was too simple to do. Forgery was always punished by death, and no mercy was ever shown to those accused of it. But where several were involved, one or two of the less guilty were told to plead 'guilty to the minor count' and escaped the death penalty. It was a sort of infernal lottery. The more guilty were condemned anyway, and many others were selected on a sort of hit-or-miss basis to die as well, just to make an example of them. Harriet Skelton had been invited to plead 'guilty on the minor count' but had not understood what this meant, and did not do so. She had not been aware that the notes were forged and did not consider herself guilty of anything.

In prison she was well-behaved, quiet and considerate, and nobody, including the other prisoners, thought that she would be condemned to die. Her case attracted much public attention and sympathy, for Mrs. Fry's reputation had begun to travel abroad: if Mrs. Fry thought she should be saved, there must, many thought, be something in it.

Mrs. Fry tried to persuade Lord Sidmouth, the Home Secretary, but he took the view that, although there were extenuating circumstances, the law should have effect and should not be changed. Mrs. Fry, who was opposed in principle to capital punishment, as she did not accept the right of any human being to take the life of another, would not let the matter rest there. She remembered the Duke of

Gloucester, to whom, with her seven sisters, she had once sung sweetly in the carefree childhood days at Earlsham Hall. Surely he would help? She approached him, and he even visited the prison to see Harriet Skelton with her, and afterwards interceded on the girl's behalf with the Bank of England and the Home Secretary. His efforts were still in vain.

In the midst of the fight for Harriet Skelton's life, Elizabeth was summoned to be presented to Queen Charlotte at the Mansion House in the City, the official residence of the Lord Mayor of London. It was a glittering spectacle. She arrived in the company of her friend and sponsor, Countess Harcourt, but owing to some misunderstanding was not presented to the Queen in the drawing-room, as had been arranged, but was placed on the side of the platform, in the vast, ornate, Egyptian Hall, to await the arrival of the royal party. After a while the Queen recognised Mrs. Fry, who seemed to stand apart, by reason of her plain Quaker dress, from all the brilliant uniforms and jewelled gowns about her. The Queen at once went up to her and greeted her; and spontaneously the great gathering clapped and applauded, and their tribute was echoed by the crowd outside. For Mrs. Fry had become to the ordinary English man and woman a symbol of mercy, a rare quality in those days, and her acceptance by the Queen seemed, to them, to imply Royal sponsorship of social reform.

Gratified as she was at such powerful backing, Mrs. Fry was still sad at heart. She thought, still, of Harriet Skelton, waiting in that cold, gloomy cell for death. All her efforts to save her were to fail. Harriet died, calmly and humbly before a crowd which at least had enough compassion not to jeer in her last moments. Lord Sidmouth, it is said, was annoyed at the pressure brought to bear on him from high quarters and was determined to show that he, and he alone, would decide these questions. Mrs. Fry's daughter, Rachel Cresswell, has described how her mother visited Harriet the day before her death: "She felt it acutely. There was something terrible to her in life being taken from one in full possession of mental and physical vigour. One woman said to her the day before she was hanged, 'I feel life so strong within me, that I cannot believe that this time tomorrow I am to be dead.'"

Is it any wonder that Elizabeth Fry wrote in her diary: "Is it for man to take the prerogative of the Almighty into his own hands?"

Prisoners of the time were considered an outcast race.

Courtesy of Mary Evans Picture Library

CHAPTER SIX

Work For The Prisoners

To reform Britain's prisons, Mrs. Fry knew, would demand several lines of action, which must be attempted one at a time. It was, after all, a complicated matter. The first need was for a penal code that would be less harsh and unrelenting. The indignity of public hanging was as degrading for the spectators - since it coarsened their feelings and rendered them immune to pity - as it was for the unhappy victim. The principle that children born in prison should be condemned to live there was palpably wrong. The business of appointing men to supervise women prisoners seemed to Elizabeth Fry, a humiliation and a needless addition to their sufferings. Yes, there was so much to do, and so much heartache - and fatigue - in attempting to do it.

Yet a start *had* been made. She had rallied round her eleven enthusiastic and influential Quaker helpers. She had focused public attention on the plight of prisoners, who had been deemed an outcast race, unworthy of thought or attention. The novel idea that criminals could respond in any degree to kindness or consideration had at least been put to the authorities, even if they found the notion too preposterous to accept. The school for children in Newgate was a success, the children being happier, better behaved and even acquiring some religious belief and at least the rudiments of education. The school had evoked in many of the women some sense of purpose, despite their wretched surroundings and their own personal sufferings. The women prisoners were clamouring for something similar to be done for them. Elizabeth Fry thought hard and long - but not too long - about it.

Of all the evils besetting the prisoners, idleness was one of the worst. In Newgate there was plenty of proof of the old adage: 'the Devil finds work for idle hands to do.' So many prisoners had committed first offences, often quite trivial ones, from mere foolishness, or impulse or pressure of poverty. Otherwise decent people, they were thrown amongst criminals of the lowest and most violent kinds, and being utterly rejected by society, themselves learned to be criminals.

Elizabeth Fry decided that the next need was for the women to be put to some useful work, so that they could retain their self-respect and feel some purpose in life. She was fairly confident that the women would co-operate, but realised that any scheme must have the approval of the authorities. Like a good strategist, she tackled this obstacle first. The sheriffs and city magistrates, and the governor and chaplain of Newgate were invited to dinner at Mildred's Court, and in a relaxed and informal atmosphere listened to the details of the scheme she had in mind. They knew, as they listened, that she was not only a woman of charm and good intentions, but of considerable influence as well, and a powerful figure in the nationwide Quaker movement, which possessed members of standing and power.

Elizabeth Fry had been presented to the Queen. She had the ear of the Duke of Gloucester. She had a large and growing public following amongst all classes. She was not a rabble-rouser, seeking to unite unruly elements of society into open or overt defiance of authority. Her useful work at Newgate had been achieved at no cost to the authorities - her own money, that of her friends, and generous sub-sidies from her brothers, sisters and relatives, had made it possible. In all these circumstances, it is not surprising that they lent a willing ear.

Her plan was simple. The women would be divided into groups of twelve, with a monitor chosen by themselves over each group. As in schools, the monitor would, of course, be the most sensible and reliable of their number, and one who could read. There should be a matron for the general superintendence of the women, and a yard-keeper, appointed by the women themselves, who would help to keep order. At nine o'clock in the morning, at the ringing of a bell, the women would collect in the workroom to hear a portion of scripture read by one of the visitors, or by the matron, and then they would disperse to their respective wards and do knitting and needlework, helped and guided by Mrs. Fry's volunteers, and in their absence supervised by the monitors.

It sounded like Utopia indeed, and many argued that the women would never submit to such discipline, least of all impose it on themselves. "I believe the women will co-operate, if the scheme is explained to them, and they are invited to decide for themselves," said Mrs. Fry, quietly. "If they agree, will you give it your approval?"

The men conferred amongst themselves. "You have our blessing and support, Mrs. Fry, if you can secure their agreement."

In company with the Sheriffs (who came so that the women prisoners might know that Mrs. Fry and her body of helpers enjoyed their full support) Mrs. Fry outlined her scheme to the assembled prisoners. Swearing, gambling, drinking, violence and idleness could never bring happiness or even relief from suffering, she told them; whatever life had done to them, they were all God's creatures and of equal worth in His sight. (She emphasised this by invariably using the pronoun 'we' in addressing them, and never 'you'.) In work there was dignity and interest, a relief from worry and a chance to learn respectable habits. Her women helpers came, not to order the prisoners about, but to help them and to impart to them the benefit of the education that they, the helpers, had been lucky enough to enjoy.

As the women listened in silence, Mrs. Fry explained the rules. There would be the matron, and the monitors whom they would choose themselves. There was to be no begging, swearing, gambling or immoral conversation. Unsuitable reading would be excluded, and any bad conduct reported to the matron. A yard-keeper, also to be elected by the women, would see rules were observed when women left their group to go to the grille and meet visitors - some of whom would often yield to clamorous begging and demands for money for drink. Work would begin after Bible reading at nine in the morning. Women would be tidy and washed. There would be a further reading at six in the evening, when the work would be handed to the matron by the monitors. The matron would keep an account of each woman's work, and of her conduct.

Mrs. Fry put each suggested rule to them separately and asked for a show of hands to indicate assent or dissent. Every one of the rules was approved, and every monitor was selected by the women themselves, each by a unanimous vote. Such a democratic procedure was, of course, nothing less than a revolution in the early nineteenth century, when the prison was regarded solely as a place of punishment..

And so the latest scheme got under way. Until it was possible for a matron to be found (and she would be paid from the pockets of Elizabeth Fry and her volunteers) the women helpers came every day to the prison and stayed all day, teaching the women how to sew and knit. Mrs. Fry persuaded textile merchants, mostly but not exclusively Quakers, to give her or sell at cost or less, scraps of coloured material, so that these could be made into patchwork quilts. The making of these was not only an interesting occupation for the prisoners - giving them scope to select which pieces they liked, and to work them to their own designs - but was also a source of profit. The quilts became a popular item of export by a city firm to overseas colonies, including Australia. They brought a touch of England to distant colonies, reminding the settlers of home. The money thus earned was saved against the day when the prisoners were released, or transported.

A month after the scheme had been in operation, the magistrates visited Newgate to see the progress made, and were amazed at the transformation. They could scarcely believe that these clean, docile women, knitting and sewing away in their neat blue aprons and bibs, were the erstwhile raving, uncontrollable social outcasts they had seen and heard only a few weeks ago. So impressed were they that they undertook to contribute towards the expense of the matron, and furnishing of her rooms. Mrs. Fry's Committee paid the yardswoman. The matron was given sufficient authority to keep order and to confine for short periods anyone who was persistently badly behaved - an authority that was not resented by the women, since the matron was their own choice, and they were anxious to keep the new privileges which Mrs. Fry and her helpers had put in their way.

So far, these privileges had been extended to the 'tried' prisoners - those who had been tried and sentenced - but there remained scores of others awaiting trial, which was often a long and tedious wait. Seeing how the other prisoners had useful means of employing their time, they petitioned Mrs. Fry's committee to be allowed to work as well, and this was arranged.

The prison authorities and city magistrates, delighted with the success of the scheme, decided to make it a permanent part of prison routine, and news of its success spread not only to outlying country districts, but to other countries as well. From all over the world letters poured in to Mrs. Fry from social reformers, lawyers, magistrates and others concerned about penal reform and the operation of law. Prisoners, instead of being a forgotten substratum of society, had at last become a topic for intelligent, though often controversial, conversation. Executions, floggings and transportations were still common but a blow had been struck at the idea, unquestioned for centuries, that cruel and savage punishments were the only way to deter criminals and discourage them from repeating their offences. Kindness as a means of regeneration had been proved, in some measure, to be effective.

News of Mrs. Fry's activities had percolated to the House of Commons, and recognising that her hopes of achieving really lasting reforms lay with those who made laws rather than with those who administered and enforced them, she gladly accepted an invitation to report to a Committee of the House of Commons concerning her work on 27th February 1818.

Quiet, demure but confident, Mrs. Fry answered a barrage of questions on every aspect of her work. Kindness worked, she told them. "Our rules have certainly been occasionally broken, but very seldom; order has been generally observed." The women, she said, feared to be brought before her more than before a judge, "though we use nothing but kindness." There had never been any petty thefts. The women were knitting from sixty to a hundred pairs of stockings a month, earning about eighteen pence for each person. The money was spent in helping them to live, and buy clothing. But her Committee, of course, supplemented their meagre earnings. "For this purpose (clothing themselves) they subscribe, out of their small earnings, about four pounds a month, and we subscribe about eight, which keeps them covered and decent."

The scripture reading, she claimed, had eased the prisoners' minds and given them new hope and self-respect. There was no attempt to expound doctrine; she confined herself to the moral principles of the Scriptures, and in any case, she explained, most prisoners were too ill-educated to assimilate or understand much more at that stage. The MPs made a passing reference to 'that woman still in Newgate whose husband was executed; and she herself condemned to death, having eight children.' The fact that eight children were to be left orphans did not seem to move them greatly; nor did Mrs. Fry press her case. There was little point in her doing so, as the power of life and death lay not with them but with Lord Sidmouth, the Home Secretary, whom she was already pressing in the matter.

In quiet, matter-of-fact manner, Mrs. Fry opened their eyes to the true state of Newgate. The prisoners ceased to be numbers: they became human beings. She described a mother-to-be who was so poor that she had to be supplied with almost every item of clothing; of another so nearly naked (her clothes had probably been seized on arrival as 'garnish') that she, Mrs. Fry, had been obliged to stand before her to cover her nakedness.

Asked "What is the average space allowed each woman to lie upon?" Mrs. Fry told them the awful truth - *between eighteen inches and two feet of space for each woman!* The moral discipline of a prison could never be complete, she assured them, until mass dormitories were abolished and each woman slept on her own. It was right that they should work, eat and have their recreation in company, but they were entitled to privacy at night. She was also opposed to solitary confinement, except 'in the most atrocious cases'.

Other points which she made at this interview were that three things were essential in a well conducted prison - religious instruction, classification (separation of the notoriously and persistently criminal from new offenders or people awaiting trial) and employment. Asked by the Committee if she thought "any reformation can be accomplished without employment?" she answered flatly, "I should believe it impossible." She made the point, too, that women should take care of women, and that the use of male warders, turnkeys and so on in women's prisons should be abolished. She pressed her point about employment, adding that it was essential to the success of the employment schemes that the women should be permitted to spend part of their own earnings, at least, on immediate necessities, such as tea and sugar.

The Report issued by this Committee gave the evidence in full, and concluded with a glowing tribute to Mrs. Fry and her workers:

"The benevolent exertions of Mrs. Fry and her friends, in the female part of the prison, have indeed, by the establishment of a school, by providing work and encouraging industrious habits, produced the most gratifying change." But much must be ascribed to unremitting personal attention and influence.

CHAPTER SEVEN

Transportation

In 1818, Elizabeth Fry found herself absorbed with the reform of yet another social evil - the transportation of female convicts to Botany Bay, in New South Wales.

This colony became a British possession in 1770. Captain Cook, who mapped the east coast of the great Australian continent, gave it that name because it reminded him of South Wales. Both Cook and his companion, Sir Joseph Banks, thought it promised well as a colony.

However such vast tracts of territory could not be made habitable and fertile overnight. Banks suggested that it would be a good idea to settle convicts there; they would be a reservoir of cheap labour, would help to develop the colony for Britain and at the same time rid the home country of trouble-makers. Once Britain had transported her convicts, from similar motives, to Virginia and the Carolinas in the American colonies until America had seized her independence and the practice stopped.

In 1787, a fleet of ships carrying 700 convicts and 200 guards set sail for Botany Bay - so called by Captain Cook because of the diversity and beauty of its plants, flowers and trees. The fleet arrived in January 1788, although this, the first shipment, was discharged at Port Jackson instead, which Captain Arthur Phillip, who was in command, thought a more suitable spot for settlement. Thus was the city of Sydney, New South Wales, founded.

Nobody saw anything very remarkable about transporting convicts thousands of miles away from their home country; huge numbers died on the voyage, and of those who arrived, hundreds found no shelter and perished of starvation or exposure. The lucky ones spent the rest of their lives on hard labour for the settlers; the less lucky laboured long hours under terrible conditions, and were flogged mercilessly for the slightest offence, such as failing to groom a horse properly or spilling some milk. At home, nobody cared. A public hardened by the spectacle of public executions, and the perpetration of constant floggings, could scarcely be expected to concern itself with what happened to convicts out of sight thousands of miles away.

Since that first shipment in 1787, the transportation of convicts had continued. Shipment included women and children, who while in prison awaiting transport, on board ship and on arrival, fared no better than the men. They were held beneath contempt; considered outside the pale of humanity.

Transportation, either for life or for stated periods (seldom for less than 10 years) could be, and was, inflicted for almost any offence, serious or trivial. It was largely a matter of caprice or chance. Sir James Stephen, a Judge of the High Court of Justice, says in his *History of the Criminal Law of England* 'that this legislation was guided by no principle whatever.' In the eighteenth and early nineteenth centuries, an immense number of Acts dealing with transportation was passed. Transportation for life could be imposed for no less than seventeen different offences. Other offences permitted transportation without specifying any period at all. Fourteen other offences carried the penalty of transportation for a *minimum* of fifteen years. Another fifteen offences could be punished by between fourteen or fifteen years. Transportation for seven years could be inflicted for twenty-three different varieties of crime. The committing of any one of nearly a hundred offences against the law could be enough to have you torn away from your home and relatives and sent, destitute of clothing, money or equipment, to far-distant Australia. The prospect on arrival was destitution or slavery. To escape from one harsh master simply meant capture by another just as cruel.

The warders at Newgate always dreaded the night before the female convicts were to be transported. They would go wild, smashing up the furniture, attacking any who came near, swearing and fighting each other, screaming and getting roaring drunk. The following day they were herded into open wagons and drawn through the streets. As they crowded together in their rags, some huddling together with a few pitiful possessions tied up in a bundle, the crowd would jeer and mock them, the children pelt them with filth and rotten vegetables. The wagons which took them to the embarkation quay at Deptford were, therefore, little more than moving pillories. They were a familiar London sight, a welcome diversion for the riff-raff of the city.

When John Howard had investigated the conditions under which transportees awaited their sentence in prison, he had uncovered the most appalling suffering. When he visited the Savoy (not the London hotel as it is now, but a former building which was then a prison for soldiers) he had found many sick and dying. In the county jail at Morpeth, in Northumberland, he discovered many awaiting transport who had, meantime, been chained to the floor for days, in such discomfort and pain that they could neither clothe nor unclothe themselves, lie down, sit up, eat or sleep.

Between 1795 and 1801, no less than 3,800 convicts were sent to Australia and in Elizabeth's Fry's time the traffic still flourished, including the cruelties to which Howard had, unavailingly, called attention.

Mrs. Fry's first step was to plead with the Governor of Newgate to send the women away, not chained together in open wagons, but in closed hackney coaches. "They dread the indignity of that last journey to the quay," she said, "and would be better behaved the night before they leave prison if only they were given this small privilege." To her great relief, her request was granted (although it did not apply to other parts of the country).

There were, of course, the usual cries of 'mollycoddling the criminals' but it meant less work and worry for the prison authorities, who on previous occasions had often had to put the women in chains and strait-jackets, or whip them.

With her helpers, Mrs. Fry visited Newgate on the night before they left, read the Bible to them, and soothed them with her calm, melodious voice.

There was something about her personality which had a calming and comforting effect on the most intractable and difficult people. Her quiet demeanour and firmness, her inability to lose her temper or to think the worst of people, have been recorded, often in the most moving terms, by those who knew her personally and observed her at work amongst the lost and rejected. Few women in history, perhaps, have earned a more touching tribute than that by Mrs. Thomas Geldart, who wrote:

"I have ... felt her soft touch, and heard the sweet tones of her melodious voice ... and I have been conscious of breathing an atmosphere of love. I have seen and heard her in large assemblies, soothing, in a manner so peculiarly her own, all that was adverse ... until her spirit seemed to rest on those to whom she spoke. I have seen her in the house of sorrow and mourning, when hearts were ready to break from sore bereavement, and the loving look was a balm... so soft, so compassionate, so thrilling...."

The prison, on the day of departure, was always a sad and moving spectacle. Mrs. Fry bustled about, helping a woman to tidy her hair here, comforting a child there, giving another a new apron, taking a message from some poor, distracted girl, the last message, perhaps, that she would ever be able to get to her parents. Prisoners who were to remain in Newgate pressed upon the women transportees pathetic little gifts, even of money, often all they possessed, and wept openly at losing their companions in suffering.

The women were quiet and orderly as they got into the hackney coaches, deeply grateful that Mrs. Fry's intervention had spared them, miraculously, the humiliation of an open ride to Deptford. Nor, like their unlucky predecessors or the women from other prisons, were they chained together.

On one occasion she saw them as far as the convict ship *Maria*, moored in the Thames, and watched with grim dismay the arrival of prisoners from other parts of the country. Thirteen women, she noted, were chained together, in such a way that when one moved all had to move; an awkward gesture by one gave instant pain to the others. She pleaded with the captain to have the irons removed; it was done. But one young woman's fetters were so small that the iron had become embedded in the flesh of her ankles, and she screamed with pain as the blacksmith knocked them off.

Mrs. Fry looked at the hundreds of women and children crammed in the ship's hold. What would they do on the long, seemingly endless voyage to Australia? What would become of them when they reached there? But she did not give way to tears, which might have relieved her but could scarcely relieve them. She thought, instead, of what she might do to make their lot more bearable.

The Captain was a good man, with no rancour towards the women. He co-operated as she outlined her plan. Each woman would have a number, so that she could be assured a place at table and a fair share of food. They were divided into messes of six each, a proposal the women welcomed, as it meant they had some assigned companions for the duration of the long voyage. They were divided, too, into classes of twelve, each having a monitor chosen from amongst their number by the women themselves.

Later, Mrs. Fry and her helpers organised the collection of scraps of cotton fabric from Manchester textile houses. And from then on, each woman convict was given a bundle of these, and also a bag containing a few personal, but vital, things - things none had the means to buy, or the opportunity. The bag contained "One Bible, one Hessian apron, one black stuff ditto, one black cotton cap, one large Hessian bag, one small bag containing a piece of tape, an ounce of pins, one hundred needles, four balls of white sewing cotton, one ditto black, one ditto blue, one ditto red, two balls of black worsted, twenty-four hanks of coloured thread, one cloth with eight darning needles, one small bodkin fastened on it; two stay-laces, one thimble, one pair of scissors, one pair of spectacles when required, one comb, one small ditto, knife and fork, and a ball of string."

In these prosperous days that catalogue of gifts may not sound very impressive; but in those days it was a treasure-trove - a passport to freedom from squalid and monotonous idleness to useful, interesting employment. During the long voyage a schoolmistress (one of the convicts) was to teach the children to read, knit and sew. Monitors would look after the Bibles, tracts and prayer-books. The women were advised to keep themselves as neat and tidy as possible, to behave in orderly fashion, set an example to the children and help to look after them, and to make useful articles, such as patchwork quilts, which would not only keep them occupied, but would earn money for them. (The women on one ship, the *Wellington,* found when their ship touched at Rio de Janeiro that they could sell their quilts for a guinea apiece).

Before the *Maria* left, the women were assembled on deck, and Mrs. Fry spoke to them. She made them feel that whatever hardships faced them, they were human beings with still much to hope for, and that God would never desert them.

It was a strange scene; the women with their pitiful bundles, standing silent and thoughtful; the curious sailors, who had climbed the rigging to get a better view, looking on; Mrs. Fry, her friends and the Captain grouped outside the cabin. She read a part of the Bible aloud, and then, kneeling on the deck, prayed fervently that Christian charity and Divine blessing might guard and protect these, God's creatures. With the tearful farewells and blessings of the women ringing in her ears, Elizabeth Fry watched the *Maria* weigh anchor and sail away.

She had - alas! - no means of controlling conditions in the country of their destination, although she was to campaign for improvements there, and kept in touch with correspondents who informed her of the bad conditions in the colony. And not every Captain, of course, was as helpful as the Captain of the *Maria*. One who had been sympathetic and helpful had died on the voyage, and his successor didn't give a button about the women. They were simply criminals to him.

But Mrs. Fry had started in motion the abolition of this evil system. She was to visit 106 transport ships and see 12,000 convicts, helping all she could and pleading and pressing everywhere for more humane conditions. Until 1843, she never lost sight of this crusade. And slowly changes for the better were wrought. Women, for instance, were no longer put in fetters.

They were allowed to breathe fresh air on deck, instead of being confined in the foetid air of the ship's hold. They wore clean and decent clothes. Later she was able to arrange that women still nursing their babies might not be transported until the babies were weaned; and they could take with them their children under seven. There had been heart-breaking scenes before, when mothers were separated from infants too young and defenceless to fend for themselves.

All this, of course, was not accomplished at once. Elizabeth Fry continued to visit convict ships until 1843, which was six years after transportation had been officially abolished, though not in actual fact. Abolition petered out between 1853 and 1864.

Elizabeth Fry's work for women sentenced to transportation not only set a completely new standard in compassion, but the publicity which attended her efforts forced it to become a topic of conversation - no longer a forgotten subject. It set the public vigorously to talking and thinking, and brought forward volunteers who agreed with her Christian principles. It rallied support for reformative measures and provided useful ammunition for those in Parliament and elsewhere who, like herself, were determined to see improvements.

Many of those wretched women, sent to Australia as a punishment, married farmers and settlers in time, and founded families which have brought distinction and progress to the continent of Australia. Some ended their lives tragically. Hundreds of women whose lives had been made happier and more useful by Mrs. Fry's efforts kept in touch with her by letter. These letters confirmed her fervent belief that few people are beyond redemption, and that cruelty degrades both the oppressor and the oppressed.

She once wrote, "The good principle in the hearts of many abandoned persons may be compared to the few remaining sparks of a nearly extinguished fire. By means of the utmost care and attention united with the most gentle treatment, these may yet be fanned into a flame, but under the operation of a rough or violent hand, they will presently disappear and be lost for ever."

CHAPTER EIGHT

Journeys And Setbacks

Elizabeth Fry was always throughout her life extremely fond of children. She understood them, and, instinctively, they took to her. As we have seen, she herself had enjoyed, in childhood, the company of eleven brothers and sisters, and the love of a devoted father and mother. She herself became mother of twelve children, eleven of them born before 1816, and the last, Henry, born in 1822. Although the pressure of her own innumerable activities, and the fluctuations in her husband's business fortunes (which later stabilised, so that he became progressively more wealthy and influential) made it necessary to place the children with relatives and in schools, she was in no sense an absentee mother. She did not pass her children on to somebody else, and forget about them. She was in constant touch with them all by letter; wrote constantly to their guardians and tutors, visited them all frequently, and often arranged reunions, when the whole family was present, at Plashet, or Mildred's Court, or Earlham Hall in Norfolk.

On the other hand, not all of her children shared her enthusiasm for the Quaker faith; a faith which seemed to one or two of them rather gloomy and repressive. In her own childhood and youth, Elizabeth herself had liked dressing in fine clothes, going to parties and receptions, and enjoyed dancing and music. All these pleasures she had renounced of her own free will, but her children had the stern discipline imposed upon them, and they were sometimes openly rebellious. Even her husband, on occasions, found her strict standards of behaviour difficult to share. To her grief, for she now considered it a misuse of precious time, he would go off to musical concerts on his own.

Elizabeth Fry's children all in their day testified to their mother's affection, constancy and intelligent concern for them. A few critics maintained that she neglected her home for her public duties, but this is not entirely just. She lived in an age when the woman's place was in the home, and a lively, active woman who crusaded for better treatment for prisoners, who visited prisons, transportation vessels, slums, lunatic asylums and hospitals, intent on improving conditions, alleviating want and doing good in a practical way was very much out of the common run. She attracted curiosity, bewilderment, and, of course, some criticism. For a great number of people were complacent and did not want to see things changed.

All the reforms achieved, not simply by Mrs. Fry but by such reformers as William Wilberforce, the slavery abolitionist (who was often in correspondence with Mrs. Fry), Robert Owen, the industrialist, who set better standards of factory employment, or Samuel Plimsoll, who campaigned against 'death trap' ships and insisted on proper safeguards for sailors, were bitterly opposed in their day.

Elizabeth Fry, whose mild manners and inability to speak a harsh word concealed a driving energy and indomitable will, was no exception. The obstinate cruelty of Lord Sidmouth, the Home Secretary, in refusing to see her or listen to her pleas for poor Harriet Skelton, condemned to be hanged on the flimsiest of evidence, is an example of the sort of thing she had to fight.

In 1818 Mrs. Fry devoted more and more time to her own family, conscious that her efforts on behalf of prisoners had made inroads into the time she could spare with her own children.

Her insight into conditions at Newgate, however, and the publicity which her efforts to ameliorate them had attracted, had in turn encouraged many other people to contact her, so she busied herself in forming Ladies' Committees, groups of well-disposed and influential women who would visit prisons in their areas, to follow her methods for improving prison life. Thus, when she made a tour of England and Scotland with her brother Joseph John Gurney, though the prime object was to attend Quaker meetings up and down the country, she made sure to visit prisons wherever she went, and to observe for herself what conditions were like and what action was needed to improve them.

She visited gaols in Durham, Haddington, Aberdeen, Glasgow, Carlisle and numerous other towns. Everywhere it was a grim story. Dunbar gaol, particularly, was a place of gloom – two small rooms reached by a narrow, dirty staircase; both rooms in a state of extreme filth, furnished with nothing more than a handful of filthy straw and 'a tub for every dirty purpose'. Haddington County Gaol was crowded, mainly because of a recent local riot. The four main cells were dark, and the floor only clay. A single tub in each cell, used for every purpose, was the only concession to sanitation. There was no warmth. One unhappy man was shackled to an iron bar and his feet kept from two to three-and-a-half feet apart by an adjustment by the warder, so that he could not rest or undress himself. In vain Mrs. Fry pleaded with his captors that his torture should be discontinued. The occupier of another cell, "an abominable dungeon", was a lunatic. In this prison no clothing was allowed in, no medical attention permitted, and no priest allowed to visit. As for the debtors, they were cramped together in a cell nine feet square and containing only one small bed.

At Kinghorn, in Fifeshire, Mrs. Fry found evidence once again of the iniquitous custom of confining mentally deranged people in prisons. One young lad had been confined there for six years, until he ended his life by swallowing molten lead.

One vicious aspect of the law as it applied to debtors in Scotland was that, in the event of their escape from prison, the jailer, and, through the jailer, the magistrate who issued the warrant for his arrest, was responsible for the man's debt. Naturally, the gaolers, refusing to take any chances of being themselves out of pocket, consigned the debtors to the most impregnable and uncomfortable parts of the prison, often in conditions of solitary confinement. Debtors were refused exercise lest they should escape. "He is kept," wrote Joseph John Gurney of this visit, "like the vilest criminal in some close, and miserable, and foetid apartment. His health is exposed to the most serious injury. Let it be remembered that respectable and virtuous persons may frequently be subjected by circumstances which they cannot control, to all this wretchedness." In other words, anyone who had the misfortune to fail in business, or suffer some other reverse of fortune which prevented him from paying his debts, would be condemned to spend his days in sickness, humiliation, loneliness and misery until death claimed him - for in this hopeless situation he had no means of raising or earning any money.

Harrowed as she was by these sights, Mrs. Fry persisted in her fact-finding tour. The wretchedness of the lunatics, in particular, appalled her. They were sick people, mentally sick, with a claim on the compassion and understanding of their more fortunate, and less afflicted, fellow-creatures; but they were treated as criminals. She had seen the man at Haddington chained to an iron bar; seen prisoners at Forfar chained to bedsteads, and some, as at Berwick, chained to the wall; but the memory of the crazed, bewildered, helpless lunatics shocked her beyond words.

The tour had been a strenuous one. Travelling by coach, by foot and on horseback, on bad roads, in all weathers, often traversing streams and negotiating dangerous paths, moving through woods and forests, across bogs or the scrub of lonely moors, through the frost or the rain or the sleet or stinging gales - Mrs. Fry had withstood all these things, as she invariably did, without complaint.

Her brother had written a book on their tour, and through their numerous connections they saw that it reached as many influential people as possible, in order that the conditions in the prisons should be talked about and discussed, and the authorities thereby shaken out of their complacency and forced to improve them.

She returned from her Scottish journey to find innumerable problems awaiting her, to tax her energy further. Her husband had had an accident and was bedridden. Her sister Louisa was seriously ill. Her diary at the time gives some indication of the strain which must have been imposed upon her depleted strength:

"My prison concerns truly flourishing; surely in that a blessing in a remarkable manner appears to attend me; more apparently, than in some of my home duties. Business pressed very hard upon me - the large family at Mildred's Court, so many to please there, and attend to - the various accounts - the dear children and their education - my husband poorly - the church - the poor - my poor infirm aunt whom I have undertaken to care for - public business, and my numerous friends and correspondents..."

At this time, too, she was greatly distressed by the suicide of her friend and fellow social reformer, Sir Samuel Romilly, who had fought in Parliament, often wholly unsupported, for some mitigation of the severe penalties for forgery. He had been grieved by the death of his wife, but Elizabeth Fry was doubly shocked, not simply by his death but from the thought that it was a sin to commit suicide. "Hardly anything appears to me so dreadful, as thus to take the work into our own hands, and shortening the precious gift of life: a more awful crime surely cannot be."

She was the subject of some ill-natured criticism, too, for allowing some members of the public to watch, when she read to the prisoners of Newgate. It had become one of the sights. Examining her conscience, Mrs. Fry decided to "do heartily unto the Lord, and not unto man; and look not either to the good or evil opinions of men." She did not want to hinder people coming to prison and seeing for themselves the good influence which kindness and religious instruction had upon these tough or simply unfortunate prisoners - it helped to prove her point that flogging and hanging and humiliation, the stock-in-trade of the authorities for so many centuries, were less effective than humane measures. The sightseers, she hoped, would go away and relate what they had seen, and so keep alive as a public issue the urgent need of prison reform. In this, she was sound in her judgment. The subject, once taboo, was now on everyone's lips, and the merits and demerits of the prison system, not only in Britain but in other countries too, attracted more and more interest. For her reputation and her published works had spread abroad.

Following a long and difficult journey to Darlington in 1819, where she was taking her two eldest boys to school, Mrs. Fry was taken ill. Weak and in pain though she was for months on end, she still continued correspondence from her sickbed.

It was while she was at Brighton that she received the grievous news that the female prisoners at Newgate had rioted again. Her Ladies Committee had continued their good work there during her illness, but her quiet, soothing presence was missed, and smouldering resentment at a number of grievances suddenly erupted.

Then the Newgate prisoners were suddenly shamed and saddened by the news that dear Mrs. Fry, "the angel of the prisons", who had taxed her own health to improve their conditions, was lying ill and had been upset by their behaviour in prison. These prisoners, including many condemned for murder, some sentenced to transportation or imprisonment for life, got together and wrote her a letter, signed by them all, which is touching testimony of the affection and respect in which she was held by them:

"With shame and sorrow we once more humbly beg leave to address you, in duty and respect to you, and in justice to the greater number of our fellow-prisoners, who through our misconduct have fallen in the general disgrace which our behaviour has brought upon us all; for which we are sincerely sorry, and entreating our sorrow may be accepted and forgiveness granted, by her, who we look up to as our most respected friend and benevolent benefactress. Entreating you to impute it to our being led away, by the passion of the moment, and humbly hoping this acknowledgement may prove successful in restoring us to your good opinion...."

The letter was signed by eleven women and witnessed by 'Mary Guy, Matron'. Mrs. Fry wrote at once from her sickbed assuring them of her forgiveness. She had been grieved, not simply because of their own situation, but because such an outbreak of disorder might discourage other authorities who had just begun to apply, or were sympathetic to, her methods of treating prisoners humanely. It might start a setback of public opinion, too. "Let me entreat you," she wrote to them in reply, "whatever trying or provoking things may happen, to do so no more, for you sadly hurt the cause of poor prisoners by doing so, perhaps, I may say, all over the kingdom; and you thus enable your enemies to say, that our plans of kindness do not answer and, therefore, they will not let others be treated kindly. Before I bid you farewell, I may tell you that I am not without a hope of seeing you before long, even before the poor women go to the Bay (Botany Bay), but if I do not, may the blessing of the Lord go with you when on the mighty deeps, and in a strange land...

For over six months Elizabeth Fry seemed to hover between life and death. At last, after lingering at Plashet, and then taking a long convalescence at Broadstairs, she returned to Mildred's Court and the hurly-burly of London.

She had not achieved her wish of seeing those unhappy rioters off to Botany Bay, but thanks to the attention which her work was attracting abroad, she did receive, out of the blue, a long and revealing letter of the terrible conditions there and of the dangers and sufferings which women transported there were to undergo. It was from an honest, hard-working Anglican parson, the Reverend Samuel Marsden who, in his own way, had been fighting a lone battle there against cruelty and bureaucratic indifference, and who now in desperation appealed to her to bestir the public conscience.

He mentioned that he had often met exiles from Britain who spoke with affection and admiration of Mrs. Fry's work for them. It was because of this that he knew he could address himself to her frankly. He was modest about his own struggles. "I have been striving for more than twenty years to obtain for them some relief," he admitted, "but hitherto have done them little good. It has not been in my power to move those in authority, to pay much attention to their wants and miseries."

When he had returned to Europe in 1807 he had submitted to the Archbishop of Canterbury a memorandum on 'the miserable situation of the female convicts.' He had addressed a similar report to the Government through the Colonial Office, and to several members of Parliament. All had promised that something would be done, that boatloads of women would not be sent to a settlement where, for example, no housing existed for them. Two years later he found that nothing had been done. Five years later again, when he protested to the Governor, he was curtly told that the Home Government had sent the Governor no instructions to build barracks.

"For the last five-and-twenty years," he declared, "many of the convict women have been driven to vice to obtain a loaf of bread, or a bed to lie upon. To this day there has never been a place to put the female convicts in, when they landed from the ships."

When the shiploads of women arrived, soldiers, settlers and convicts went aboard and took possession of any women they liked, treating them as slaves. With nowhere to go, the women were forced to accept any conditions that offered. This evil had continued unabated for *twelve years* after the Rev. Samuel Marsden had informed the most influential people in Britain, including members of Parliament and the Government itself, of the evils rampant in Botany Bay.

As usual, Elizabeth Fry lost no time in acting on this new information. Why, here was she and her fellow volunteers, struggling to convince female convicts that the world cared about them and that they would start a new life, and authority was sending them into exile in conditions which made it certain that a large proportion of the transportees could exist only by crime and vice. Ceaselessly she badgered authority, and the barracks were, eventually, built.

Of course, the building of the barracks (at Paramatta) did not make New South Wales a paradise for these unfortunate women. Women disembarked at Sydney, were taken up-river to Paramatta and there housed in a prison called the Factory. Good conduct prisoners usually found employment with settlers, who might treat them well or badly, as they pleased. If they were treated badly, and many in fact were mercilessly ill-used and even flogged, they had no redress; for any insubordination or bad behaviour they could, on the uncorroborated complaint of an employer, be returned to the prison. However, the building of the barracks was at least the beginning of an improvement, and Elizabeth Fry had long since learned that in achieving reform one must 'make haste slowly'.

CHAPTER NINE

Help For The Homeless

In all her endeavours Mrs. Fry had constantly in mind that her mission was to live as her God would wish. There was no thought of self. She hob-nobbed with the rich and influential on equal terms mainly because through their financial, moral and political support she could gain general acceptance for her ideas and secure the adoption of her principles by the authorities themselves. Again and again, an examination of her voluminous journals testifies to her constant self-examination, a continual watch for selfishness or ulterior motive.

Yet she could delegate. She did not seek the limelight herself, but could scarcely avoid it because her reforms seemed so revolutionary and far-reaching during her lifetime. Her first thought always was - where can I find others to do what I consider worth doing? She was an able organiser, and knew the value of picking the right people and then trusting them to do what was required without irritating criticism or needless supervision.

Whenever she visited a prison she always went to see local magistrates, and any influential friends in the district, and persuaded them to form a Ladies Committee charged with visiting the prisoners and applying the principles of Biblical reading, employment for the women, and separation from the men.

Following the success of the Newgate Committee, too, she had formed a Corresponding (we would say Correspondence) Circle, to answer inquiries from interested people who were willing to help but were inexperienced in the work, and to assist other districts to form similar committees. So the beneficent work spread.

Always the same principles were emphasised concerning prison reform: female prisoners should have privacy at night instead of being herded together; they should be classified, that is, separated with some regard to their characters and records, so that those who had committed first offences were not brought under the baneful influence of hardened, impenitent criminals; that there should be unceasing superintendence, instead of the bad old habit of locking everyone up and virtually ignoring them; that they should be supervised by women and not by men; that some occupation should be made compulsory, so that they were not the prey of despair and idleness; that there should be provided regular education and religious instruction for them.

Apart from these prison activities, which gathered momentum all the time, Mrs. Fry could not avoid being caught up in other philanthropic activities. She was, for example, one of the first people to establish a Provident Society - once such a feature of modern society - by which people saved for such things as buying a home, paying for illness or emergency, and for retirement. When she had been ill at Brighton, she had received so many requests for help that she had formed a Brighton District Society with the Bishop of Chichester as patron.

This Provident Society had two main aims: relief of distress and the teaching of self-help to the poor. For although distress of all kinds was rampant in those days, it must also be admitted that much of the suffering was due to the low standard of literacy then prevailing. The Society's committee members would visit the poor in their homes, relieve genuine distress, whether in the form of sickness or poverty, and encourage 'industry and frugality'. For in those days, as in these, there were problem parents as well as problem children. For too many workers drink was the only refuge from the appalling factory conditions, and their meagre wages, insufficient in any case to keep a family decently, were squandered on drink. Savings banks were formed so that such people could be encouraged in thrift.

Mrs. Fry was a pioneer in two other social movements which still flourish and do useful work today: a movement for the after-care of discharged prisoners, and another for help and guidance of juvenile offenders.

She had often found that young prisoners, held for short sentences, had nothing to hope for on being released but a reversion to crime. It was quite impossible in those days even to hope to secure employment without a first-class reference from a previous employer, which was never given if someone had a brush with the authorities, however slight. In any case, many prisoners, released penniless to live and with nothing to eat, were by mere desperation - as well as disposition - to break the law again.

With such a long list of offences on the statute book punishable by death, it was clear to Mrs. Fry that something should be done for such people before it was too late. And so she opened shelters for discharged prisoners in Dublin and Liverpool, and another in Westminster known as the Tothill Fields Asylum (we associate the word 'asylum' today with institutions for people who are mentally ill, or with refugees from oppressive regimes; the word means literally 'refuge' and was used in that sense then).

Mrs. Neave, a wealthy woman from whom Mrs. Fry sought support for her scheme, placed on record the immediate effect of Mrs. Fry's eloquence and personal magnetism. "Often have I known," Mrs. Fry had told her "the career of a promising young woman, charged with a first offence, to end in a condemned cell. Was there but a refuge for the young offenders, my work would be less painful." These refuges were a radical departure from tradition, which had held that those who broke the law had themselves to blame for the consequences, even if these were out of proportion to the offence.

Juvenile crime in the nineteenth century was very prevalent. Those were not the days of compulsory education. There were scarcely any laws to protect children against the neglect of their parents, or ill treatment by them or their employers. Hours of labour were in practice unregulated. Home conditions were often as bad as they could be - filthy, crowded, ill-lit slums, devoid of privacy or the facilities for keeping clean and tidy. There was nowhere to play but in the streets.

Children began to earn their living far younger than they are permitted today. Very small boys were employed in the fields to scare birds by waving a rattle, women and children worked underground in mines - some of the latter scarcely out of infancy. Indeed, when the Mines Act of 1842 decreed that women and girls must no longer work in mines, and that boys could not work there until they were *ten,* an outcry went up that the working class was being mollycoddled! In factories it was usual to find children of seven or even younger working over twelve hours a day, even on Sunday, when they were made to clean the machinery. They were freely beaten to keep them at work. Apprentices, often parish children, deserted children, or orphans, kept alive on the barest minimum of food and invariably farmed out as apprentices at the earliest possible age, were little better than slaves. They were not paid for their labour. Their hours were unregulated. They slept in dirty and uncomfortable quarters in the factory itself.

Except for a handful of people such as Mrs. Fry, the plight of Britain's children was regarded with what seems to us today a quite incredible indifference. How was it possible, when in 1817-19, Henry Grey Bennett, the Radical Member of Parliament for Shrewsbury, tried, by petitions and Bills in Parliament, to abolish the use of small boys as chimney sweeps, that he could have been so obstinately opposed? That some of these children were as young as five years, that most contracted the most horrible skin diseases through scraping their skin constantly against jagged brickwork or stone as they squirmed their way through dark, sooty labyrinths; that some had become jammed, and suffocated; that employers lit straw or stuck pins into the soles of their feet to get the boys moving - all this seemed quite normal.

Bennett's humane bill was thrown out and the evil persisted for decades, despite an Act of 1840, which theoretically at least, was intended to restrict it. Sweeps simply ignored it, and not until 1864 did the Earl of Shaftesbury, the well-known Victorian reformer and philanthropist, succeed in getting a Bill passed by which, *on the Statute,* sweeps were prohibited from taking boys into houses at all. The practice was rife when Charles Kingsley described the "climbing boys" in *The Water Babies* in 1863. Only Lord Shaftesbury's further Bill of 1875, which made it compulsory for sweeps to apply for licences, which could be refused if they used boys, really ended this scandal.

In other words, despite Bennett's evidence of tragedy and suffering amongst chimney boys, given in detail in 1817, children were condemned to go on suffering under that iniquitous system for well over half a century before anything was done about it.

This, then, was the climate of opinion in which Elizabeth Fry so bravely lived and worked.

The improvement of factory conditions, too, was an equally slow business, and in her time the conditions could only be called slavery. Robert Southey, the poet, declared, "The slave trade is a mercy compared with it." The tremendous increase in the number of power looms in Britain - from 2,400 in 1813 to 14,500 in 1820 - had created a demand for cheap labour.

It was illegal to strike for better working conditions or wages; compositors working on *The Times* were sent to prison in 1810, under the Combination Laws, for striking. If children, or adults for that matter, were injured in the factories, as they often were, they were not entitled to free medical treatment, or compensation of any kind. William Blake, the mystic and poet, did not exaggerate when he wrote, in hatred of the system, of "those dark, Satanic mills".

The low wages paid to labourers meant, inevitably, that many could not support their families, and that infant mortality was very high. Jonas Hanway, the social reformer, had said that few parish children lived to be apprenticed. How tragically true this was is illustrated by the story of Captain Coram, a kindly sailor who, touched by the plight of the thousands of abandoned children, started the Foundling Hospital to provide a refuge for them. In due course the Government decided it should be made available for all abandoned and homeless children - without, however, increasing its accommodation or resources proportionately. Of 15,000 children brought there under this cruel and thoughtless edict, only 4,400 - less than a third - lived to be apprentices.

The fact that these, and many other, evils were in due course remedied, and that England was the first country to introduce such reforms as the abolition of slavery and effective factory legislation, should not blind us to the real nature of the suffering which existed before these could be achieved, or the courage of those who exposed, and fought, these evils at a time when authority and often the mass of people themselves were indifferent, or callous.

When Elizabeth Fry returned to London after her long illness, and threw herself once more into the round of Quaker meetings, prison visits and welfare work, there were thousands of homeless children wandering the streets of London.

It was one of the worst winters London had known for years, and one young boy was found frozen to death in the streets. With the help of her husband, the members of the Ladies' Newgate Committee, kindly friends, Quakers and relatives, a meeting was called, money collected, and a 'nightly shelter for the homeless' was opened in a large warehouse in London Wall, the building being offered free by Mr. Hicks, a kindly tradesman of Cheapside.

In these days its comforts seem limited enough - a gaunt, empty warehouse, with straw for the men and boys to sleep upon, and a little bedding for the women and girls. But there was bread and soup for all who needed it, medical help for the sick (Mrs. Fry was always a good nurse, and easily taught others the rudiments of tending the sick and dying) and clothing for those in rags. This was paradise compared with the open streets. Every night over 200 people, and often as many as 800, flocked there for refuge.

CHAPTER TEN

Other Causes

Wherever Elizabeth Fry went, she thought of what she might do to lessen unhappiness, no matter what the cause. Despite the fact that she consistently over-worked, and was a prey to nervous exhaustion brought on by having too many cares on her mind at the same time (during the last twenty-five years her health progressively declined), she never turned away a chance to do some constructive good. Even if she lacked the necessary money herself she would badger those who had it.

Once, while taking a ride on the south coast near Brighton, she came across a lonely coastguard. When she spoke to him he told her, politely, that he was not allowed to speak to anyone and, to save him getting into trouble, Mrs. Fry gave him her visiting card with a request that he give it to his commanding officer, thus making it clear that it was she who had attempted to talk to the man, and not the other way about.

As a result of this encounter she received a visit from a young naval lieutenant, and from him learned of the lonely, dangerous and ill-paid life of over five hundred coastguards. Disliked by the local inhabitants, and by the smugglers against whom they had to defend the shores, segregated in lonely, inaccessible places and cut off from human society most of the time theirs was a very miserable life.

Though little could be done for them, that little was valuable. Mrs. Fry organised a supply of books and Bibles to the five hundred coastguard stations, so that the long days of boredom, and the lonely evenings, could be spent enjoyably and usefully. She managed to extract a grant of £500 from Sir Robert Peel, Secretary for State and founder of the 'Peelers' - the first policemen to patrol the highways of London. This in turn led to two further activities - the provision of books for lonely shepherds, and libraries for the women and children on convict ships.

Next, Mrs. Fry undertook a comprehensive tour of prisons in Nottingham, Lincoln, Wakefield, Doncaster, Sheffield, Leeds, York, Durham, Newcastle, Carlisle, Lancaster, Liverpool and many other towns. By now she had streamlined her plan of campaign. Always calm, deliberate and imperturbable, she would make herself known to the magistrates and local authorities, who opened all doors to her.

Once inside the prison, she spoke freely with the governor, the turnkeys and the prisoners, inquiring closely about every detail and inspecting every inch of the prison. Nothing escaped her. She would then set about forming a Ladies' Committee, who would visit the prison on lines similar to those of the Newgate Committee, organising reading and classes, seeing that the women were occupied, and generally helping the prisoners. In due course she would compile a detailed report on the prison and send the prison authorities a copy of it, in order that they could never claim they didn't know what was going on in their own prisons. Details were also published in the annual reports of the Society for Improving Prison Discipline, so that they might be read by its many influential members, including the Duke of Gloucester, and sympathetic members of Parliament.

Prisons everywhere in the world were at that time in a disgraceful state, and reformers in other countries naturally wrote to Elizabeth Fry asking how she went about things and what methods they should follow. She welcomed such correspondence, although it was an added burden. Through Mr. Walter Venning (and, when he died, through his brother John) Mrs. Fry extended her influence to Russia, where Ladies' Prison Associations had been formed in St. Petersburg after the pattern of the Newgate Society. The Emperor of Russia, ladies of high rank and Prince Galitzine followed Elizabeth Fry's correspondence with the liveliest interest.

She explained how Ladies Associations were now established throughout Britain, how women convicts were under the supervision of monitors and a paid matron, how the monitors organised lessons and kept a class book. "It is wonderful," she told her Russian friends, "to observe the effects of kindness and care upon some of these poor, forlorn creatures." Mrs. Fry heard with joy that the Emperor Nicholas and the Dowager Empress had visited a lunatic asylum, observed the terrible conditions there, and straightway ordered the Government to purchase a palatial house with two miles of garden and a pleasant stream - the Emperor defraying part of the cost.

She was delighted to learn that the Russians had adopted her suggestion that lunatics - except for the violent ones - should dine together. Former methods of serving the food had been most disgusting. Mrs. Fry had told them that serving food decently helped insane people to keep their self-respect, while those who were only temporarily insane were more likely to recover by being treated kindly than as if they were wild animals, with their food almost thrown at them. So, to their joy and surprise, the St. Petersburg lunatics found themselves at last in decent surroundings, and their food served on a table with a clean tablecloth, and plates and spoons.

Mrs. Fry's insistence on the usefulness of Bible reading was touchingly confirmed by the correspondence. "I have witnessed a poor lunatic, a Frenchman, during an interval of returning reason, reading in his bedroom the New Testament, with tears running down his cheeks," Mr. Venning wrote to Mrs. Fry, "also a Russian priest, a lunatic, collect a number together, while he read to them..." Whatever Mrs. Fry wrote to Mr. Venning he would translate into French for the Empress; and she, having read it, would order it to be translated into Russian and delivered to the Asylum as an order.

And so, in this amazing way, Elizabeth Fry could reach out, often from her sickbed, to ease the sufferings of far-distant Russians who had never heard of her. A similar co-operation existed with the Danish royal house. The Prince and Princess Royal of Denmark, during a visit to England in 1822, had met Mrs. Fry, the Princess had breakfast with her at Plashet, and a friendship commenced which lasted for the rest of her life.

Indeed, as the years progressed, she found herself in correspondence with all the crowned heads of Europe. She was not content with simply giving advice and hoping for the best. In the course of subsequent travels (for which she was constitutionally unfitted, becoming easily exhausted), she was to inspect prisons in France, Germany, Holland and many other countries, in each case making recommendations - which were later put into effect - for the alleviation of the prisoners' suffering.

It was, perhaps, inevitable that a woman of Elizabeth Fry's unique personality should have found life harder and harder as she grew older. As her strength declined, so her activities grew, for she could never refuse an appeal for help, and one activity simply led to another. Her activities as a Quaker minister, too, were very demanding, often calling her to as many as four or five meetings a week, in places often widely separated. And her family circle, despite the deaths of relatives and their children, grew constantly. In November 1822, she became a grandmother and a mother on the same day: bearing her eleventh child on the day her married daughter, Rachel, bore her first child.

It is not surprising that she wrote, in 1823: "My occupations are just now multitudinous. I am sensible of being, at times, pressed beyond my strength of body and mind…" And again in 1825, during a spell of her recurrent illness: "I feel so unfit, so unworthy, so perplexed, so fearful, so sorrowful… but I believe . . . that out of this great weakness I shall be made strong."

These confessions, however, were written in her private journal; because she was an exacting person, demanding much of herself, frustrated when her strength gave out, anxious that she should not be wanting in courage or unselfishness. In circumstances of danger and discomfort she often behaved better than many men. Like Grace Darling and Florence Nightingale, she was a woman with woman's instincts and yet brave as a man. This combination of courage and genuine humility was, perhaps, the secret of her ability to come instantly to terms of understanding and mutual trust with anybody, from a convict woman half-crazed with grief and fear to a king head with power and wealth. No one failed to succumb to her spell.

An incident which shows her character was related by Captain Martin who, in 1821, was in command of the Ramsgate Steam Packet, the *Eagle*. He ran into a thundery squall while racing two rival steamers when, about two miles from Purfleet, he saw Elizabeth Fry and a friend, in their Quaker habits, being buffeted about in a boat which was out of control and now struggling against a powerful tide. He rescued them, took them on board, and as the gale cleared Mrs. Fry was on deck, cool and collected as she offered religious tracts to the sailors, with a sidelong glance at the Captain to 'see if he approved.'

"Who," said the Captain, "could resist this beautiful, persuasive, and heavenly-minded woman? To see her was to love her; to hear her was to feel as if a guardian angel had bid you follow that teaching...".

On that occasion, she had been visiting a convict ship. On a similar mission, on another occasion, she had gone to see Admiral Young at Deptford, to ask permission to visit a ship. It was pitch dark, squally and pouring with rain, and seeing her so tired and strained he appealed to her to remain with his family until conditions were better. To this she replied that one of her children was seriously ill, and she wanted to get back home as soon as possible. The Admiral and his family were greatly moved. This woman, with all the worries of nursing a sick child at home, had still braved the appalling weather to visit and comfort some unknown convict women before they sailed away into pitiable exile.

In 1827, Elizabeth Fry set out on a tour of Irish prisons, lunatic asylums and hospitals: she also paid pastoral visits to Quaker meetings in Ireland. She had left her children in the motherly care of Catherine, her eldest daughter, at their Plashet home, and travelled with her brother, Joseph John Gurney and her husband's sister, whose name was identical with her own - Elizabeth Fry. At Lisburn, the huge crowds, curious to catch a glimpse of the famous reformer, pressed upon her so closely that she was in danger of being suffocated. At Londonderry they were greeted by a peal of church bells. She attended the crowded meetings, or sat with humble peasants in their turf huts while the chickens fluttered around them. She hurried from meeting to meeting and from prison to prison, until, at Waterford, she became seriously ill. After a rough channel crossing she arrived to learn that her sister Rachel was also seriously ill, and went straightway to her old childhood home at Earlham to comfort and nurse her.

Then came an ordeal which was to scar her for the rest of her life. Her husband's business failed, and he went bankrupt. The complete collapse of their fortunes not only meant that they must leave Plashet - the country home they had grown to love - but that she now had the worry of finding a home to live in, the distress of dismissing servants who had served and loved her, the worry of how to provide for her huge family, the responsibility of supporting and consoling her husband in his misfortune and, worse still for her, the awful wrench of handing over such charitable projects as had, hitherto, been financed largely from the pockets of herself and her husband. The schools for the poor at Plashet had to be handed over to another helper, William Morley. Bailiff's officers invaded her home, making an inventory of their furniture and possessions - many of them treasured family possessions - prior to their sale, to satisfy the creditors.

All this was sad enough to the Quaker banker and his wife, who had poured out their money and their time on every charitable cause; but worse was to come. The Quaker community regarded severely those of its members who failed in business: its strict standards are understandable when we remember how many unsound business speculations in that age brought financial loss and misery not only to the promoters but to creditors and investors. The Yearly Meeting had recorded that if any Friends "by their failure bring open scandal and reproach on the Society, then Friends justifiably may and ought to testify against such offenders." The tragedy was not that Quakers in an age of commercial laxity, economic distress and keeping up with the Joneses set high standards for their members, but that they administered regulations with an indiscriminate harshness.

Moreover, there were in Joseph Fry's Meeting a few rather grim, austere types who had long regarded Fry's comfortable standard of living, and his love of music, with a baleful eye. There were probably a few, too, who resented and envied - some had openly criticised - Mrs. Fry's prominent social connections, which she valued mainly because they conferred on her a hearing in influential (and therefore effective) quarters when seeking to get unjust laws changed, or alleviating the miseries of the unprivileged and dispossessed. Mr. Fry, who had been in no sense dishonest but rather the victim of economic misfortune, was disowned as a member of the Society at the very moment when he and his wife were most in need of sympathy and support, when they were already staggering under the financial blow.

The incident simply hardened the Fry children in their resolve not to be Quakers. Mr. Fry, bitterly resentful, put aside his Quaker clothes and refused to wear them. Yet Mrs. Fry's journal, while revealing what she describes as "anguish of the spirit", has little trace of bitterness and shows no wavering of the faith in God which had impelled and sustained her through so many trials and struggles. "When I look at this mysterious dispensation permitted by Almighty wisdom," she wrote, "I am ready to say, How is it, Lord, Thou dealest thus with Thy servant, who loves Thee, trusts Thee and fears Thy name? ... I cannot reason upon it, I must bow... and say in my heart.... 'Not as I will, but as Thou wilt.'"

Elizabeth Fry's friends did not desert her. Letters of sympathy flowed in, from Wilberforce, the slavery abolitionist, now an old man with failing sight; from Mrs. Opie, widow of the artist who had painted Elizabeth and her sisters when they were girls; and from many others. Relatives provided them with sufficient money to live modestly. After staying for a time at their old home in Mildred's Court with their married daughter Rachel, they went to live in a house at Upton Lane, near the home of Sam Gurney, Elizabeth's brother.

In due course Joseph Fry paid all his private debts, and years later was reinstated to Quaker membership; but he neither forgot nor forgave the slight to his good name. Elizabeth continued to wear the habit, the severe cloak and bonnet, and to observe the rules and discipline of the Society. Her deep-rooted piety was unshaken, even though she knew, in her heart, that the movement included some who were too concerned with external things, such as how to dress and how to conduct meetings. Some, perhaps, were a little more anxious to detect and expose faults in other members, whereas Elizabeth Fry had a more positive approach. There was a difference, she thought, between merely avoiding sin and actively practising virtue. The first was necessary but in itself it was not enough.

CHAPTER ELEVEN

An International Figure

Elizabeth Fry bore her changed mode of life philosophically. There were fewer lavish dinners, fewer servants and she travelled by ordinary stage-coach instead of in her private carriage. Gradually her husband recovered his position. Although beset (as she was throughout life) with innumerable family demands, Mrs. Fry still maintained her activities in the Quaker movement; and she continued with her reform work, for whereas some of her ideas had been adopted in places such as Newgate, there were still many black spots in the other parts of the country.

She had already witnessed great changes in her lifetime. The remote arrogance of the landed gentry, for so long indifferent to the sufferings of the labouring classes, was now challenged by many reformers. The idea that factory workers should be simply industrial slaves, underpaid, over-worked, badly housed and denied freedom either to change their job or organise together to secure better conditions, was on the way out. Slavery in the colonies, although still flourishing, was vigorously challenged by such men as William Wilberforce and Sir Thomas Fowell Buxton. In 1829 the streets of London, teeming with thugs and rogues, were made a little safer by the appearance of the uniformed police.

By the time William IV ascended the throne in 1830, reform in all spheres of life was being talked about. The success of the Whig majority at the General Election in 1830 ushered in what is now known as the Whig Reform Period. Statesmen began to realise that the fear of revolution (George the Third's reign had been notable for ugly riots, some within earshot of Elizabeth Fry's home) was lessened by improved conditions; they found that the labouring classes were becoming vocal, and had, furthermore, influential champions. The argument that any attempt to improve social conditions must fail because the poor were pre-destined to be poor and ignorant had been disproved by Elizabeth Fry with her prison work, and by Lord Shaftesbury in his battle against destitution.

Battles for improved conditions are seldom won overnight. Slavery is a case in point. In 1823 Thomas Fowell Buxton (he had taken over the leadership of the Abolitionists from Wilberforce) had welcomed the Government's proposals for 'effective and decisive measures' for making the lot of slaves less harsh. The Colonial Assemblies were given copies of the British Government's resolution, but refused to accept its proposals. An Order in Council, made in 1824, laid down a new and detailed code of improvements, but this, too, was treated by slave-owners with contempt.

It is not surprising to find, therefore, that when Mrs. Fry called on the Duchess of Kent and Princess Victoria (later Queen Victoria) she "took some books on the subject of slavery, with the hope of influencing the young Princess in that important cause."

Nor did Mrs. Fry let the matter rest there. She had talked to Princess Victoria in May 1831, but the following month, in connection with a sale of work she had helped to organise to finance a hospital ship on the River Thames, she met the Queen and other members of the royal family, and discussed slavery again. Such was her reputation, and her charm, that she could afford to raise these highly controversial topics at such meetings. Nor did she hesitate to do so.

She knew, of course, from her anti-slavery friends that the old evils persisted in the colonies. As a matter of fact, even the Abolition Act of 1833, a first step towards total abolition of slavery, never worked satis-factorily, even though it was valuable as showing a changed attitude in Parliament. Under it, children below six were to be freed at once, other slaves were to work as 'apprentices' for seven years, and £20,000,000 was to be paid as compensation. The distribution of the money was wholly unsatisfactory: 'apprentices' were still treated as slaves, and ill treatment still occurred. It is one thing to make a law and another to enforce it - particularly when thousands are making money out of breaking it. It was only the persistence of people like Mrs. Fry which kept public attention focused on this subject, and pressed the Government into seeing that those laws were actually obeyed.

After five years of such campaigning by the Abolitionists, the Colonial Legislatures abandoned the apprenticeship scheme (which had too often proved merely the continuation of slavery under another name), and agreed to the outright, immediate emancipation of all slaves. It had been a long and hard fight.

In 1833 Elizabeth Fry, who had so much occasion, over the years, to record tragedy and suffering in her private diary, was able to admit to herself that her years of endeavour were bearing fruit. From the outset, even at the age of seventeen, she had tried to do good wherever she could. But there was a difference, as she well knew, between isolated acts of kindness and mercy - important though these were - and a *general* improvement in conditions. She had always tried to work for both; to alleviate immediate distress as much as her physical and financial resources, or those of her supporters, would permit, and, at the same time, to press for some positive action to prevent such suffering in the future.

Now she could be sure that, although so much remained to be done, the pendulum was definitely swinging towards social reform of every type, and she was able to note in her diary: "The suppression of Slavery - the diminution of Capital Punishment - the improvement in prisons, and the state of the poor prisoners - the spread of the Scriptures, also of the Gospel to distant lands - the increase of education and knowledge generally, and many other things, are truly encouraging."

This same year she visited Jersey for her health, but, as usual, made it her business to know the inhabitants, ask about their problems, and help where she could. With her husband, children and friends, she wandered about the beautiful island, always with her little bag of religious tracts, always in her severe Quaker clothes, with her face, ageing a little now, still alight with piety and love. Her knowledge of the local patois - inherited by the inhabitants from their Norman ancestors - was not perfect, but instinctively the people of Jersey liked her. She would sit in their humble cottages, round the stockpot suspended over a fire of dried seaweed, and talk to them of her faith, and of the importance of love and trust in human relationships.

But, as usual, she made a point of visiting the hospital, the workhouse and lunatic asylum and the prison, and when she left addressed to the authorities in Jersey a lengthy memorandum setting out her comments and suggestions for improvement; the separation of men from women, of hardened criminals from trivial offenders, a standard and adequate diet, prohibition of alcoholic drinks, decent prison-dress, a clear code of prison routine and discipline, the need for employment and the importance of religious instruction. In this report she made the telling comment that the gaoler was paid only according to the number of people his prison contained! Naturally, he kept everyone there as long as possible, while others were *induced to come in!*

Her note was important, as the island was not subject to British law. But her recommendations, once so novel but now an accepted part of the law in most enlightened European states and the United States of America (as well as the UK) were duly noted and later acted upon. We think of a hospital today as a place wholly devoted to the alleviation of pain and suffering, but she mentions a woman who, having been discharged from prison, was sent as a further punishment to *hospital,* where for several weeks she wore a heavy leg-chain attached to a log, night and day. It is scarcely to be wondered at that Mrs. Fry suggested that the hospital could be improved upon! She commented adversely, too, upon the arrangements in the lunatic asylum; safe custody, and restraint by force (which was often cruel and brutal) were still the main preoccupations of the attendants. The buildings, she insisted, were only suitable for "violent, incurable, or outrageous patients."

Besides maintaining active contact with reformers in Russia and Denmark, Mrs. Fry helped and encouraged people like herself in similar endeavours in other countries. She corresponded frequently with Dr. Julius in Berlin, who put into effect many of her principles regarding prison reform - as, also, did the Marquis de Pastoret in France. Another recruit to Mrs. Fry's ideas and ideals was the Marquise de Barot in Italy, who had started a refuge for fallen women in Turin.

Mrs. Fry's Prison Discipline Society - which had developed and gone from strength to strength as a result of her efforts to improve conditions at Newgate as far back as 1813 - had achieved its greatest legal victories, which were of course victories for the ordinary public, in the passing of such Acts of Parliament, as 4 Geo. IV. c. 65 and 5 Geo. IV. c. 85, between 1823-4. These Acts had, at least, given legal weight and approval to the principles she had advocated so strenuously, such as the need to preserve the prisoners' health, improve their morals, keep them employed, and the abolition of the use of chains in all but the most violent and intractable cases.

Mrs. Fry did not believe in solitary confinement, which had often been inflicted as a punishment on some prisoners for years on end. Even debtors, especially in small county jails, were often subjected to this abominable treatment, being confined for years on end in damp, dark and unventilated cells, completely inactive and with nobody to speak to and nothing to read. Not surprisingly, many lost their reason under such treatment, and Mrs. Fry maintained that it was more cruel to deprive a man of his sanity than it was to mistreat his body - although both were bad.

Mrs. Fry believed in *segregation* of prisoners, that is, their imprisonment in separate cells, because this kept the less guilty from being contaminated by hardened, impenitent criminals (and there were some very tough and remorseless characters in those days, as there are today). But, subject to their classification into groups, such as first offenders and persistent criminals, she had always insisted on their working together, exercising together and eating together. Separate confinement at night, of course, was to ensure that rowdy prisoners would not keep others awake, and that illicit drinking, rowdyism and fighting, which were such a feature of Newgate and other prisons in the bad old days, could not occur.

All prison discipline, as it existed in 1830 and onwards, could be said to be based on Mrs. Fry's humanitarian ideas. Gaol fees were abolished, 'garnish' done away with, the appointment of chaplains to prisons was compulsory, and improved prisons were built, embodying the features which she advocated. Millbank Prison, begun in 1813 and partly completed in 1817, had been opened with much publicity, and was governed by a specially appointed Committee, the Chairman of which was the Speaker of the House of Commons.

Between 1832 and 1835 Mrs. Fry appeared before Committees of both the House of Lords and the House of Commons, and described her work amongst the prisoners, the destitute and the delinquent. Increasing respect and interest were being paid by all sections of the public to her ideas. And it was necessary that public opinion be enlightened, since although Millbank had been built as a model, as an example of how a prison should be constructed and run, its example could not be forced upon local authorities. Some showed enterprise and humaneness, and built new prisons, others persisted in their bad old ways. Only the force of public opinion could bring about change. New county jails were built in such places as Derby, Penzance and Leicester, while prisons such as Yarmouth and Barnstable improved existing premises and varied their prison routine in accordance with more modern ideas.

This was not a period in which a law could be passed by Parliament and its intentions be instantly achieved throughout the country. Nowadays, of course, a central government can make laws and see that they are applied with equal effectiveness throughout the country, with local authorities (such as Borough Councils, Urban District Councils and Rural District Councils) concerning themselves with local government problems in full conformity with general laws and general policies.

But this stage of stream-lined efficiency was achieved only after centuries of trial and error, and of conflict between Whitehall and local authorities. Until the end of the sixteenth century local authorities were hardly concerned with anything but the upkeep of roads, bridges, prisons and county buildings, and even then these were (since 1555) under the supervision of justices of the peace.

In 1601, under provisions of the Poor Relief Act, parishes were given power to levy rates on the inhabitants, and use the money so collected for the relief of destitution in their areas, and were required to appoint unpaid officers to carry out the executive work. Justices of the Peace, too, were to supervise this work. We know that "poor relief" was of the most frugal kind, and that the destitute, sick, mentally ill, the aged, homeless children and orphans ere often kept, when they were kept at all, on the brink of starvation. It was not much better in Dickens's time.

From the passing of the Poor Relief Act, the development of local government was a slow business. Justices did as they pleased with virtually no control from anyone. Too often municipalities used the money collected as much for their benefit as for that of the inhabitants - hence the deplorable conditions of most county gaols. Innumerable separate authorities, such for example as the Turnpike Trusts (which maintained stretches of road and charged users a fee) added to the administrative confusion. The result was described by one writer as "a chaos of areas, a chaos of franchises, a chaos of authorities, and a chaos of rates." Citizens had no right to elect members of such Councils, or supervise or control the expenditure of public money, or policy, in any way.

The Parliamentary Reform Act, in 1832, extended the general franchise to the middle-classes, such as farmers, shopkeepers and professional men, giving them a voice at last in the election of Members of Parliament, but the working class were still refused a voice in affairs. The Poor Law Amendment Act of 1834, however, divided the country into groups of parishes called Poor Law Unions, each under a Board of Guardians, placing central control in the Poor Law Commissioners. The Municipal Corporations Act reformed local government in over half the boroughs, by preventing many abuses, extending the vote to rate-payers and controlling local expenditure by the introduction of a borough audit system. The administration of justice was separated from local affairs at last. Even so, county authorities were left untouched by the new legislation, and remained under the control of justices, many of them aged, corrupt or just lazy.

That was why it was necessary for Elizabeth Fry to continue to press for reforms in certain prisons, despite the fact that the Acts passed in the reign of George IV laid down that certain things should be done. That is why, wherever she went, she made a point of visiting the local prisons, asylums and hospitals, so that she could point out their deficiencies to those who ran them and to other authorities (including the government as well). She might, one would have thought, have got awfully tired of continually repeating the same recommendations. In the cause of humanity she did not tire.

CHAPTER TWELVE

Continental Travels

From 1838 onwards Elizabeth Fry spent much her time travelling on the Continent, to spread the Gospel (she never went anywhere unless laden with religious tracts and Bibles for free distribution), to attend Quaker meetings, to propagate her ideas on prison reform, to campaign against slavery, to plead for religious freedom and the merciful treatment of religious minorities, and to inspect and advise on the organisation of social services generally.

Travel was a great strain on her, involving as it did rough Channel crossings and long, often bumpy journeys in stage-coaches in all weathers, and she was frequently taken ill along the way. Did she sense that her days were numbered? Occasionally, in her journal, she laments her failing strength, but remains as convinced as ever that, sustained by the help of God, no harm would attend her until she had completed her mission. Far from curtailing her many activities (as her husband continually asked her to do, from anxiety for her health) she pressed forward with her campaigns more determinedly than ever.

Her labours in Britain, and the heavy demands of her enormous family, had prevented her from travelling abroad until late in life. In any case, this delay had been an advantage to her cause abroad, because her reputation had gone before her and she was received, by both high and low, with respect and enthusiasm.

In 1838, accompanied by her husband and two friends, she made a tour of France, holding receptions for notable people, visiting prisons and similar institutions, and reading the Bible to prisoners and helping to form Ladies' Committees along similar lines to those in England. As usual, she sent a voluminous report of her findings and recommendations to the Prefect of Police before leaving the country.

In the same year she visited Scotland, and, appalled at the continued practice of solitary confinement in prisons there, called a meeting of over fifty people, including magistrates, lawyers and members of the Prison Discipline Society, to plead for some mitigation of what she had always, and still, regarded as one of the cruellest of punishments.

In the following year she visited France again - this time with her husband, her daughter Catherine and a friend.

The year 1840 began happily. Queen Victoria, who had ascended to the throne three years before, and whom Mrs. Fry had visited as a Princess, sent her fifty pounds as a donation to the Refuge for Young Offenders in Tothill Fields. Soon after this, she left with her brother Sam and three other Friends for a long and exhausting tour of the Continent.

This tour, which was repeated again in 1841, has been described as 'a crusade amongst the prisons and institutions of Belgium, Holland and Germany'. Certainly Mrs. Fry found plenty of scope for improvement in the prisons and institutions she visited. At Ghent she inspected a prisoner's cell which was more like a torture chamber than anything else; the floor and walls were made entirely of pointed triangular pieces of wood, so that the wretched occupant could neither sit, lean against the wall, nor lie down without excruciating pain. Nor, of course, could he sleep either. At Antwerp she was depressed by "a prison in a deplorable state, where much evil, I fear, is going on."

At the prison for women at Gouda, twelve miles from Rotterdam, she found over three hundred female prisoners under the supervision of only two women and five men. There was no supervision of any kind at night.

Worse was to come. At Hamelin, in the Kingdom of Hanover, she found four hundred prisoners, heavily chained. One "tall, fine figure with heavy chains on both legs, sat weeping like a child." At

Hildesheim she visited another terrible prison in which "poor, untried prisoners" were chained to the ground until they confessed their crimes whether they had committed them or not. She discussed these and other matters with the prison reform societies, and also presented a petition to the King on the persecution of Protestants, in which she pleaded for more religious tolerance - despite the advice of the British Ambassador that this might give offence. (As it happened, it did not.)

Her 1841 journey with her brother Joseph John Gurney included Holland, Germany, Prussia and Denmark. She met the Crown Prince of Prussia, who was deeply impressed by her sincerity, while on a visit to the Danish court. While brother Joseph harangued the King of Denmark, Mrs. Fry was pleading with the Queen for the "poor Baptists in prison". She never hesitated to plead for religious toleration, even when the oppressed minorities were not followers of her own Quaker faith.

Later in 1841 Mrs. Fry witnessed a distressing demonstration of the harm which can be inflicted by solitary confinement. Visiting a convict ship, she found several women mentally deranged after such confinement. "This must lead me," she said, "to make further and stronger efforts for an entire change of the system adopted with them." The next year, following ugly scenes on the convict ships *Surrey* and *Navarino,* she pressed hard for the appointment of matrons to accompany the female convicts on board another ship, the *Garland Grove,* which was taking 205 women to Van Diemen's Land. Eventually no such ship sailed without one or two matrons to attend to the women's needs and keep them in order.

When, in 1842, Elizabeth Fry was invited to the Mansion House in London - official residence of the Lord Mayor - to meet Prince Albert, the Queen's consort, the Duke of Wellington and various Ministers, her first thought was: *what good can I do by going?* Great banquets and ostentatious displays of wealth ill-accorded with Quaker austerity. But she went. To the Consort she spoke long and earnestly on the need for religious education, the state of religion in Europe as she had observed it for herself, the state of the prisons in Britain and the danger of punishments becoming too severe. This last subject, too, she discussed with Sir Robert Peel.

Whenever a new prison was built Mrs. Fry made a point of seeing it; and even before it was built she was usually consulted about the plans, so that she could point out any disadvantages in the design. At this time Pentonville Prison, commenced in April 1840 and completed in 1842, was a topic of lively discussion. It had cost £100,000 to build, upon the plan of Lt-Col. Jebb, with whom Elizabeth Fry had been in correspondence. She maintained that some of the cells were too dark. The prison covered an area of nearly seven acres. Each cell was nearly 14 feet long and 7 feet broad, and was provided with a water-closet, pail, wash basin with water, and a slung hammock with mattress and blankets. The exercise yard was so constructed that the prisoners could be easily observed.

For its time, Pentonville was a model prison. It embodied many of Mrs. Fry's improvements and was a tremendous advance on the dark, filthy, overcrowded prisons elsewhere. It was adopted by the Government as a pattern for all provincial prisons within their control. Two years earlier Mrs. Fry had visited Parkhurst Prison, in the Isle of Wight, and had been able to record in her journal: "One day I visited Parkhurst, an interesting new prison for boys, which gave me much satisfaction. It was curious to see some of the very things that in early life I in part began, carried out in practice. I have lived to see far more than I expected of real improvement in prisons."

On the other hand, there was the Penitentiary (later called the Millbank Prison) on the northern bank of the River Thames, between Westminster and Vauxhall Bridges, the largest prison in Britain, covering 16 acres and used mainly for prisoners sentenced to transportation. It had 1500 cells, 40 staircases, over three miles of corridors, and had cost over £500,000 to build - a tremendous sum in those days-and showed the tremendous difference in the Government's attitude of mind since Elizabeth Fry's early days, when any old building would do. There was talk, of course, of mollycoddling the criminal, but actually the discipline at Millbank was very severe, and its conical-roofed towers earned it the name of 'the English Bastille'. Of its punishment cells, one writer wrote:

> "The dark cells, twenty steps below the ground floor, are small, ill-ventilated and double-barred; and no glimpse of the day ever enters this fearful place, where the offender is locked up for three days, fed upon bread and water, and has only a board to sleep on."

It is safe to assume, therefore, that Sir Robert Peel did not get very much chance to enjoy his food at the Mansion House banquet! "I expressed my fears," Mrs. Fry wrote, "that gaolers had too much power, that punishment was rendered uncertain" *(i.e. capricious, and therefore unjust)* "and often too severe-pressed for the need for mercy, and begged him to see the new prison and to have the dark cells a little altered."

Though she personally shrank from publicity, Elizabeth Fry spared no opportunity to bring her cause before the public eye. When the King of Prussia visited England in 1842 (she had met him, as Crown Prince, during one of her Continental tours) she arranged that he should visit Newgate Prison. The prisoners must indeed have realised their plight was not forgotten when Elizabeth Fry, accompanied by the King, the Lady Mayoress and Sheriffs of the City of London entered the prison yard. Mrs. Fry read to the prisoners in her usual manner, and then, with complete simplicity and lack of self-consciousness, knelt down and prayed for the prisoners and all assembled there. She left upon the arm of the King, who later dined with the Frys' at their house at Upton Lane, in company with her eight daughters and daughters-in-law, seven sons and eldest grandson.

From now on Elizabeth Fry's intermittent illnesses became more frequent and more severe. Against advice, she insisted on visiting France again in 1843 with her brother Joseph John Gurney, despite the terrible channel crossing, during which many passengers begged her to abandon the journey and return home. She managed to visit old and new friends, and visit prisons, including the evil St. Lazare - "such a scene of disorder and deep evil I have seldom witnessed" - and returned to battle with Lord Stanley, Secretary of State for the Colonial Department, for improved conditions for female convicts in New South Wales.

But she was past battle. For over forty years she had taxed her strength beyond endurance. She had worried about everybody and everything and had striven so hard to ameliorate the lot of the dispossessed, the inarticulate, the lonely, the homeless, the sick, the insane and the wicked (none of whom she ever admitted to being beyond redemption).

Dogged by fatigue and stress, she was taken to various resorts - to Sandgate, Cromer, Ramsgate – in a vain attempt to recoup her vanished strength.

At Ramsgate her health grew worse. With an immense effort she managed to attend a Quaker meeting. When she returned she asked, in a curiously solemn way: "Are we all now ready? If the Master should this day call us, is the work completely finished? Have we anything left to do?"

And then, even more solemnly: "Are we prepared?" A few days afterwards she was near her end. Her husband and children tended to her few wants and read frequently to her from the Bible. On the morning of 25th October, 1845, one of her daughters was reading from it when Mrs. Fry, who had seemed almost in a sleep, roused herself a little and said, slowly and distinctly, "Oh! My dear Lord, help and keep thy servant!"

Elizabeth Fry, the angel of the prisons, had spoken her last words.

Before a vast crowd, and attended by her family, the body of Elizabeth Fry was laid to rest in the Friends' Burying Ground at Barking. She had been conveyed from Ramsgate to her old home, Ham House in Upton Lane, and through the grounds of Plashet House, where she had known so many happy days. As the company gathered round the grave they were enfolded in the reverential silence of Quaker worship, and it was her most-loved brother Joseph John who despite his grief first lifted up his voice in thankfulness to God for her life, and who towards the close fell upon his knees in prayer.

Elizabeth Fry had struggled hard and long for reforms which were partly achieved whilst she lived, and mostly achieved afterwards. The prison system today, with its numerous safeguards for the individual, is based fairly firmly on the principles she so boldly advocated at a time when such proposals were novel and revolutionary.

Not only had she written mercy into the pages of the Statute Book, but she had brought some degree of happiness into the lives of thousands of people during her lifetime. Many tributes were paid to her, both during her life and afterwards.

After her death a little gift arrived, addressed to her, from a convict woman who had been transported in 1823. She was Hester, one of Mrs. Fry's school-mistresses, chosen from among the prisoners at Newgate. When she had left Newgate to go on her long exile abroad, Mrs. Fry had pressed into her hands a pound of lump sugar and half a pound of tea. Except for Mrs. Fry, she hadn't a friend in the world. But Mrs. Fry had given her hope, as a result of which she had begun a new life in New South Wales. Now she wrote to say that she had been married twenty years, adding with pride that she had "plenty of pigs and fowls; buys her tea by the chest; and the patchwork quilt which now covers her bed was made of the pieces given her by the ladies when she embarked." She sent Mrs. Fry, as a present, a calabash (the fruit of a tree, dried, cleaned and made into a bottle) which, in its simple way, was as eloquent and effective a tribute as the statue of her which now stands in the Old Bailey in London.

Women were often hanged for trivial offences.

Courtesy of Mary Evans Picture Library

SOME ELIZABETH FRY DIARY ENTRIES

Elizabeth Fry kept a copious diary. It has never been published in full. The following are some extracts.

Year: 1797

July 10th

Some poor people were here, I do not think I gave them what I did with a good heart. I am inclined to give away, but for a week past, owning to not having much money I have been mean and extravagant. Shameful! Whilst I live may I be generous, it is in my nature; and I will not overcome so good a feeling. I am inclined to be extravagant and that leads to meanness for those who will throw away a good deal, are apt to mind giving a little.

July 11th

I am in a most idle mind and [intend] to have an indolent dissipated day; but I will try to overcome it and see how far I can – I am well, oh most inestimable comforts. Happy, happy, me to do so well how good, how virtuous ought I to be! May what I have suffered be a lesson to me, to feel for those are ill and alleviate their sorrows as far as lays in my power; let it teach me never to forget the blessings I enjoy. I ought never to be unhappy; look back at this time last year how ill I was, how miserable; yet I was supported through it; God will support through the suffering he inflicts; (....) I could fall on my knees, and be most grateful for the blessings I enjoy, a good father, one whom I dearly love; sisters formed after my own heart, friends who I admire and good health which gives a relish to all. Company to dinner, I must beware of not being a flirt; it is an abominable character; I hope I shall never be one, and yet I fear I am now one a little. Be careful not to talk at random. Beware and see how well I can get through this day without one foolish action. If I do pass this day without one foolish action it is the first even passed so, if I pass the day with only a few foolish actions, I may think it a good one.

July 27th

I have been thinking I am now in a most uncertain state, I shall either turn out a flirting worldly woman, or I may be a virtuous, interesting woman; may I never be one, and may I be the other; but I fear for myself inexpressibly lately I have loved the world too well, I will; as one of the seven sisters be good, and let my heart glow with the warmth of enthusiasm.

August 12th

I do not know if I shall not soon be rather religious because I have thought lately what a support it is through life; it seems so delightful to depend upon a superior power for all that is good; it is at least always having the bosom of a friend open to us (in imagination) to rest all our cares and sorrows upon what must be our feelings to imagine that friend Perfect, and guiding all, and everything as it should be guided. I think any body who had real faith could never be unhappy; it appears the only certain source of support and comfort in this life and what is best of all it draws to virtue and if the idea be ever ill founded that leads to that great object why should we shun it? Religion has been misused and corrupted, that is no reason religion itself is not good. I fear being Religious in case I should be Enthusiastic.

Year 1799

December 5th (EF's thoughts on her betrothal to her husband)

This day my father had a letter from Joseph Fry saying he intended being here next (second) day – now this letter has led me to serious thought, and I believe I might have seen my right path ... I believe the true state of my mind is as follows, I have almost ever since I have been little under the influence of religion, rather thought marriage at this time was not a good thing for me – as it might lead my interests and affections from that same in which they should be centred, and also if I have any active duties to perform in the church. If I really follow as far as I am able the voice of truth in my heart, are they not rather incompatible with the duties of a wife? And a mother? And is it not selfish to wait and see what is the probable course I shall take in life before I enter into any engagement that affects my future life?

Year: 1800

July 15th (the Public declaration of an intention to marry that is made by the members of the Society of Friends in their monthly meeting).

I think I have been rather blessed through the proceedings of the day, I felt calm not much dreading what I had to pass through, I was low the first part of the meeting for worship, but my feelings were clam about the affair. I was agitated without painful feelings. In the women's meeting I spoke boldly and cryed; (afterwards) I was much calmer, altogether I have had a comfortable and cheerful day.

November 11th After marriage

I feel there are many weeds to root up. But I must remember my old doctrine not to look too much at the mountain before me but look only to my present steps, that I may not only *look* forward, but try to be *getting* forward. My Joseph and myself seem to unite in a mutual wish for obtaining good, that sympathy is pleasant. It seems to me that I am unusually near the fountain of good this night oh may I lay in a stone against the day of temptation.

Year: 1801

February 3rd

This morning after writing notes I walked out and went to see a poor woman who I half like and half do not as there is something in her very odd. However, I spent much time about her. I then read the letters from home which were comfortable and satisfactory. (….) I was just dressed for company. We had a pleasantish visit, but I think of late I more and more dislike society of every kind; I really wish for a more retired life; my present constant liability to company seems too much for my weak mind.

February 7th

I am almost surprised when I see how little I go on with my employments; how little quiet I have with my husband; indeed how much of my life slips away without seeming to do hardly any thing (….) But when I look at my daily interruptions I do not much wonder. It has not a pleasant or good effect on the mind (….) My thoughts are now very often in my nursery, [dreaming up] plans for children (if ever I should have any) – I am very full of castles about my good management but all must be should be held in subserviancy to a great and divine power, who alone knows what is best for them and us, and it is to be hoped He will in His mercy guide the hands of the parents, to lead them in the right path in every way. I am a great friend to close and constant attention to early education, even the very first years of a childs life.

May 5th

What a great pity it is I am so much afraid of other people

December 12th After the birth of her first child

After reading I dressed baby, got her to sleep and sat down to write letters which I did till somebody called, I was then busy with baby till time to dress for dinner; how very little I do! I have got into the habit of procrastination and idleness; for much of my time is spent in doing little, and the rest I am obliged to be in great hurry to get on at all; so I go on, *dead* and flat as to religion and religious.

Year: 1802

March 3rd

Since tea I have been writing to Kitty, sitting with my dearest Joseph, and getting my little one to sleep. I long to live more quietly at home for I do not think much order or regularity can exist in so unsettled a state as our own; for I think we have hardly had a quiet month since we married. My Joseph talks of going in to Norfolk and leaving me which I think will be both odd and dull.

August 13th

I have been very anxious for fear a lukewarm state has taken some possession of us both, which I feel very dangerous, I have felt many fears and discouragements, but hope; my faith is very weak at times I fear I give way to mistrust.

I should think it ensure morality among the lower classes if the scriptures were oftener and better read to them. I believe I cannot exert myself too much, there is nothing gives me such satisfaction as instructing the lower classes of people.

Year 1825

April 12th The Frys are threatened with bankruptcy

We almost stand in fear every hour, whether we can stand the very awful storm in money matters.

September 12th

Our present state appears to be this, that we have nearly exhausted our resources, and without further assistance our stopping payment appears (humanly) speaking almost certain – we have for some time thought ourselves more than able to pay everybody. Now this is questioned by our nearest friends, and if as they think, then I understand they mean to do no more. This is a very awful condition to be in – I have seen too much of the [serious results] produced by such downfalls. It is not simply the fall in life and the perplexity attending it, but I know the pain of falling into the hands of men, however good, or however dear. Once dependent, the difficulty of pleasing those on whom we depend, is so very great... The prospect in the evening of our day of losing all our outward possessions, and many of our comforts is certainly very serious, and the way in which our dear children may be cared for, but I think us part so trying as the perplexity of mind … the loss and suffering brought upon many others by these things, and the current of evil repost upon all the poor sufferers. This is the sad side of the question if this trial should be permitted us; but, the source of consolation is this, that a kind Providence knows what is best for us, and can overrule all for our good, and even make a way of escape for us, if right; and secondly however ill things outward may fail, may we yet know it to be out meat, and our drink to do or to suffer according to our Master's Will, and He may be pleased not only to bless the dispensation to us, but to all who may suffer by us; if any should suffer.

…. I doubt not I want a shaking, my tender body has appeared to require even me comforts and indulgences of life, and of late I have particularly enjoyed them. I might have nested in them, and my many outward enjoyments in this sweet place and the general outward prospects of our family.

November 28th

Still a time of trial and anxiety in business. My mind much ruffled by it yesterday, but in tender mercy after seeking for help, the storm was gradually quieted and became a calm. How many ups and downs of life have I known! But if I sought for Grace, sufficient was found to sustain in every state.

CRITICAL BIBLIOGRAPHY

Roy Porter's *English Society in the 18th Century*, 1991, provides an uproarious and compulsive read, while also providing the most scholarly survey of the period's social history. There is no better guide to the ideas of the period than the same author's *Enlightenment: Britain and the Creation of the Modern World*, 2000. In *The Origins of Modern English Society, 1780-1880*, 1969, Harold Perkin shows how industrialisation brought about a social revolution, which had profound implications for the atrophy of Elizabeth Fry's work in the nineteenth century. The paucity of progress since is all too apparent in Stephen Tumim's *The Future of Crime and Punishment*, 1997. Louis Blom-Cooper's *The Penalty of Imprisonment*, 1988, shows how far Elizabeth Fry's warnings about the dehumanising effects of solitary confinement continue to go unheeded. Further evidence may be found in numerous volumes of *The Howard Journal*. The effects of the incarceration of female prisoners are particularly disturbing, as Jo Deakin and Jon Spencer show in their 'Women behind bars: explanations and implications', *Howard Journal*, vol. 42, no. 2 (May 2003) 123-36. Although Gordon Rose's excellent *The Struggle for Penal Reform: The Howard League and its Predecessors* was written as long ago as 1961, his depressing account of the situation then, has become even gloomier today. Mick Ryan's *The Acceptable Pressure Group: inequality in the penal lobby: a case study of the Howard League...*1978, supports Gordon Rose's view that enmeshment in the Establishment is the inevitable price to pay for The League's influence on penal legislation.

As Elizabeth Fry drew so much of her inspiration from her beliefs as a Quaker and on a practical level derived considerable moral and material support from her co-religionists, the following works on the

Quakers are strongly recommended: A. Neave Brayshaw's, *The Quakers: Their Story and Message*, 1927, still offers one of the best introductions; On their role in Society, see Richard Tilman Vann's *The Social Development of English Quakerism, 1655-1750*, 1978; On the important contribution of Quakers to the Industrial Revolution, a very useful introduction is Arthur Raistrick's, *Quakers in Science and Industry: Being an account of the Quaker Contributions to Science and Industry during the 17th and 18th Centuries*, 1950; a more up-to-date account is to be found in *Business and Religion*, ed. D.J.Jeremy, 'How Quakers coped with Business Success: Quaker industrialists, 1860-1914', by T.A.B. Corley; see also Hodgkin, ed., *Quakerisn and Industry*, 1938

As evident throughout Dennis Bardens' text, Elizabeth Fry's standing as a feminist has been grossly ignored. Useful correctives are: Jane Rendall's *The Origins of Modern Feminism: Women in Britain, France and the United States, 1780-1860*, 1985. More focused on the period and on England is Frank Prochaka's *Women and Philanthropy in nineteenth-century England*, 1980. A claim that Elizabeth Fry, far from being a conservative religious philanthropist, was a feminist far in advance of her time, as a pioneer in 'caring power' is convincingly argued by Annemieke van Dreath and Francisca de Haan in *The Rise of Caring Power: Elizabeth Fry and Josephine Butler in Britain and the Netherlands*, 1999.

Ideas on penal reform were transformed by Michael Ignatieff's *A Just Measure of Pain: The Penitentiary in the Industrial Revolution, 1750-1850*, New York, 1978, in which he showed the refinement of cruelty in the hands of the bourgeois state. In S. Cohen and A. Scull's *Civil Society and Total Institutions*, Ignatieff in chapter 4 revises some of his earlier opinions. Michel Foucault in *Discipline and Punish*, 1975, explores the psychological implications of modern penology. A very readable survey of changing attitudes to crime is Christopher Hibbert's *The Roots of Evil: a social history of Crime and Punishment*, 1963. Those who feel that the churches have received insufficient recognition for their contribution to penology will find this lack made good in Harry Potter's *Religion and the Death Penalty in England from the Bloody Code to Abolition*, 1993.

On the need to rekindle the reforms of Elizabeth Fry today, Louis Blom-Cooper's *The Penalty of Imprisonment*, 1988, is warmly recommended. For the best informed insider's account of prisons today, read: Stephen Tumim, *The Future of Crime and Punishment*, 1997. On the Howard League for Penal Reform, a useful introduction is Gordon Rose's *The Struggle for Penal Reform: The Howard League and its Predecessors*, 1961, in which he provides a convincing case for the League collaborating with the establishment, if 'with a long spoon'. Mick Ryan in his *The Acceptable Pressure Group: Inequality in the Penal Lobby: A Case Study of the Howard League and RAP*, 1978, adopts the same view.

Elizabeth Fry, who did so much to bring out the best in the female prisoners of Newgate, has also cast her beneficial spell on her biographers. John Kent in his *Elizabeth Fry*, provides a helpful analysis of the appalling prison conditions with which Elizabeth Fry wrestled, but fails to give sufficient weight to the religious ideas, which clearly inspired her work. June Rose in her *Elizabeth Fry*, 1980, makes her subject live as a woman, a wife and a mother, without, however, really placing her religion in its vital social context. Biographers quarry their material primarily from Elizabeth Fry's many writings, even if few can make her live with the vivid touch of Dennis Bardens. The chief source is naturally the forty-six extant volumes at The Friends House in Euston Road of her *Diary*, a 'soul book', in which she recounts her spiritual experiences, rather than everyday events. The *Diary* is condensed intelligently, with the addition of other material in *Memoir of the Life of Elizabeth Fry, with extracts from her Journal and Letters, edited by Two of her Daughters* [Katharine Fry and Rachel Fry], 2 vols, 1847. Elizabeth Fry's ideas on prison reform are set out in her *Observations on the Visiting, Superintendence, and Government of Female Prisoners*, 1827, to be found at The Friends' House on Euston

Road, along with her other works, including those listed below. Sir Thomas Fowell Buxton, the slave abolitionist, who succeeded William Wilberforce and was Elizabeth Fry's brother-in-law, wrote *An Inquiry, whether crime and misery are produced or prevented by our present system of prison discipline, 1818.* In it there is a detailed description of Elizabeth Fry's work. A moving contemporary report on Elizabeth Fry, as a prison reformer, can be found under 'Active Benevolence' in *The Hangman*, vol. 1, no. 4, Boston, Wed. Jan. 22, 1845.

Life in Elizabeth Fry's mileau.

Courtesy of Mary Evans Picture Library

THE RELEVANCE OF ELIZABETH FRY FOR TODAY – A PERSONAL VIEW

Based on a conversation with Dennis Bardens, 10 June 2003. Dennis was intending to write about the relevance of Elizabeth Fry to the modern prison service but unfortunately was incapacitated by his final illness. Adrian Smith spent an afternoon with him beforehand discussing this.

Elizabeth Fry was a Quaker – a Christian group who look for something of God in everyone they meet and do not see anyone as totally evil or irredeemable. Since the days of religious persecution in the seventeen century, when many Quakers themselves were put in jail, they have always been concerned for prison reform and an approach to offenders that would lessen the likelihood of future wrongdoing, rather than exacting revenge.

Elizabeth Fry approached the women prisoners in Newgate as a fellow mother, appealing to them to consider the welfare of their children. Her work has a particular relevance today. The UK currently sends a higher number of its citizens to jail than any Western country, except the United States. Judges and magistrates are putting more people behind bars, and imposing longer sentences. Prison numbers are higher than they have ever been, and are expected to go on rising. Though far fewer women than men are sent to prison, the number of women prisoners has risen steeply in recent years, though there has been no increase in female offending which could account for this. Two thirds of these women have dependent children at home. Separating children from their mothers is well known to be a decisive factor in creating a new generation of young criminals, yet sentencers do not appear to let this fact influence their decisions.

ADRIAN SMITH - *Quaker, and author of 'Coldharbour'.*

OBITUARY OF DENNIS BARDENS

Dennis Bardens, who has died aged 92, played a brief, but crucial, role in broadcasting history as the founding editor, in 1953, of BBC Television's *Panorama* programme, then a news magazine. He was also a friend and encourager of the occult artist Austin Osman Spare. Many of the books that Bardens was later to write concerned magical subjects, on which he was an acknowledged expert. The disparate character of these achievements gives some clue to his protean nature.

Bardens was born in Midhurst, Sussex, the son of an army major and an actor. His mother deserted him and went to Australia when he was three, and his father was often away on military duty. Bardens did not get on with his siblings, so he had to fend for himself at Portsmouth grammar school, which he left early.

After serving a newspaper apprenticeship in Cardiff, he made his way to London in the late 1920s, with the intention of becoming a poet. He soon joined the bohemian and occult circles gathered around Victor Neuberg, the great disciple of Aleister Crowley - whom Bardens once met - and discoverer of Dylan Thomas.

It was through Neuberg that Bardens met Spare, whose works are now highly regarded, but who was then living in squalor on the Walworth Road, in south London. They became great friends, and, shortly after the Second World War, Bardens organised an important exhibition of Spare's work. Spare subsequently painted several portraits of Bardens.

Meanwhile, Bardens was proving himself as a journalist, working, during the 1930s, for the *Sunday Chronicle, Sunday Express* and *Daily Mirror*. In 1940, he became a distinguished reporter of the Blitz. After discharge from the Royal Artillery on medical grounds, he spent two years with the Ministry of Information, and was in charge of coordinating plans for newspaper services in Britain in the event of a German invasion. In 1943, he was transferred to liaison work with the Czechoslovak government in exile, which included, at the end of the war, secret service work in Czechoslovakia.

After 1945, Bardens worked on periodicals published by Odhams Press for three years, and, in 1949, was appointed editor of the BBC radio documentary series *Focus*. However, *Panorama*, the product of his subsequent move into television, was not, at first, a great success, and, after six months, he moved on to work, initially, for the Foreign Office and then for commercial television, at the inception of ITV in 1955.

In later life, he was mainly a freelance television editor, writer and journalist, distinguishing himself as a royalty watcher and occultist, and with 15 books to his name, ranging from *Churchill In Parliament* (1962) to *Ghosts And Hauntings* (1965) and *The Lady Killer* (1972), about the French multiple murderer Dr Landru.

Bardens had a lifelong interest in psychical research, and was a life member of the Ghost Club Society. He was also a member of International Pen, the Society of Authors and the National Union of Journalists. A man as sharp as he was kindly, as mischievous as he was portentous, he was an indefatigable *coureur de femmes*, and was the centre of a vast, vivid and sometimes quarrelsome circle which, despite a whiff of the aristocracy, was essentially democratic.

Bardens was always vigorous in defending his right to be acknowledged as the true founder of *Panorama* and, at the programme's 50th anniversary celebrations last year, he spoke movingly about those long-past events, with which the official Panorama history, by Richard Lindley, fully credits him.

Essentially a self-made man, he had all the passionate enthusiasm and volubility of the autodidact. Hard-nosed newspaperman, occultist, mason, clubman, spy, writer, man about town, Bardens's roles were infinite and, although he talked about every aspect of his existence at disarming length, he retained a core of mystery.

He was married to the former Marie Marks, who predeceased him, as did their son Peter (obituary, April 8 2002), a rock keyboard musician.

Dennis Conrad Bardens, journalist and occultist, born July 19 1911; died February 7 2004

C.A.R. HILLS
SATURDAY FEBRUARY 21, 2004 -
THE GUARDIAN

A PERSONAL RECOLLECTION OF
DENNIS BARDENS BY C.A.R. HILLS

I first met Dennis Bardens when he was in his late eighties and I was in my mid-forties at a rest home for artists in the Surrey countryside. Dennis was exceptionally bright, and ready to entertain me with more stories of his extraordinary past. Did I know that he was the founding editor of *Panorama*? That he had been the great friend of Austin Osman Spare? That he had met Aleister Crowley? What about his wartime exploits in Czechoslovakia? I was suitably impressed. Our mercurial, rewarding friendship had begun.

To know Dennis was to enter a fascinating social world, composed of people from many different backgrounds, and of different colours and creeds, because Dennis, although he had all the normal prejudices of someone born in 1911, was no respecter of persons. It was to visit his charming, totally old-fashioned mews house in Notting Hill, to be given splendid lunches at friendly local restaurants, to attend the parties of the aristocracy, to be borne off to Margate, to partake of dinner in the Edwardian ballroom of the St Ermin's Hotel with characters who seemed if possible even more legendary than Dennis himself.

Dennis did not stand for any nonsense. He became ill with terminal cancer, and I visited him when he was very weak at his flat. I found myself looking for important files in his room and being roundly told off because I failed to produce the right one. When even more ill, there was a plan that he should enter a hospice. At this excellent institution they were used to the sweet gratitude of the dying patients. But Dennis's plan to use the place as his private office quickly made them reconsider whether he would be a suitable resident.

I had to try and repay Dennis for his generous hospitality. He came to at least one, perhaps two, of the annual birthday parties to which I invite all those who have invited me. He arrived looking frail on the arm of two friends and a magnificent raffia armchair was soon found for him outside my door. He didn't stay there long, but started moving round, talking the hind leg off a donkey. But, though one of the world's champion talkers, Dennis was not really a monologist. He was too shrewdly interested in other people for that.

He spent a long time in the Phoenix Ward of the Saint Charles's hospital, where the nurses were so kind to him. I went to visit him there at the Christmas of 2000. I thought this might be his last Christmas. How wrong I was! I had got slightly lost and arrived just before the patients' suppertime. The staff allowed me to share the ward's meal. I couldn't just take it free. They suggested I buy a raffle ticket. A few days later I received a phone call. I had won the top prize, a magnificent Christmas hamper. I lack the taste for whisky. I was able to donate the Glenfiddich to Dennis.

Dennis's 92nd birthday party was an event that nobody present will forget. Somehow Joyce, (*Publisher's note: Joyce has been the help and mainstay of Dennis's last years, a trusted confidante for well over a decade. Preparations for their marriage were well advanced when Dennis was overtaken by his last illness. Joyce will hopefully forgive mention here that Dennis was very much a ladies' man. A great humourist, he would habitually answer the telephone with the words: 'God's Gift to Women here!'*) had managed to get him back from the hospital to the house in the Notting Hill mews. The room was immensely crowded with his myriad friends. It was very hot. He looked as if he was about to expire at any moment. The ambulance was quickly summoned and Dennis was carried triumphantly down into the mews where an anxious crowd had assembled. Would we ever see him again? Would he die before he even reached the hospital? From the ambulance, as the rain began gently spitting in the summer evening, Dennis gave us an oration like a dying Roman emperor. Then the doors were slammed shut, the ambulance departed amid our cheers, and we returned to the wonderful party.

But Dennis did not die on that occasion, as he had not done on so many previous ones. Now we were at the Christmas of 2003. He was near the end now. They had taken him from the Phoenix Ward to the Hammersmith Hospital for emergency treatment that would save his life. I caught him there, as he was just about to return. Still the unexpected conversation flowed on, this time boyhood memories of the wonderful food that used to be available in the early 1920s. The porters approached. I had decently to leave. We had only a moment. He quoted from the *Book of Kings*. These were the last words he said to me. I think I've got them almost right. "Since it was in thine heart to build a house for the Lord, thou didst well that it was in thine heart." And I left feeling that I had received a blessing.

NOTES

1. William Purcell, *Ten Social Reformers*, 1987, 17
2. Annemieke van Dreath and Francisca de Haan, *The Rise of Caring Power: Elizabeth Fry and Josephine Butler in Britain and the Netherlands*, Amsterdam, 1999, 64
3. *The Hangman,* vol 1, no. 4, Boston, Wed. Jan. 22, 1845, 'Active Benevolence', 1
4. Elizabeth Fry, *Memoir of the Life of Elizabeth Fry, with extracts from her Journal and Letters,* ed. by two of her daughters (Katharine Fry and Rachel Fry), 2 vols., 1847, vol. 1, 9
5. *Ibid.* 8-9
6. Roy Porter, *English Society in the 18th Century*, 1991, 119-21
7. Annemieke van Dreath and Francisca de Haan, *op. cit.*, 30
8. Arthur Raistrick, *Quakers in Science and Industry: Being an account of the Quaker contributions to science and industry during the 17th and 18th centuries*, 1950, 17-19
9. *Ibid.* 335-337
10. Jane Rendall, *The Origins of Modern Feminism*, 1985, 73-75
11. *Ibid.*, 93-94
12. Mary Thale, 'Women in London Debating Societies in 1780', *Gender and History*, vol. 77 (April 1995) 5-24, 10-12
13. Jane Rendall, *op. cit.*, 231
14. Harry Potter, *Hanging in Judgment: Religion and the Death Penalty in England from the Bloody Code to Abolition*, 1993, vii
15. Dreath and Haan, *op. cit.*, 70
16. *Ibid.*, 18
17. Mary Thale, *op.cit.*, 20
18. Roy Porter, *op. cit.*, passim, esp. 58ff.
19. Dreath and Haan, *op. cit.*, 73

20. *Ibid.*, 51
21. Frank Prochaska, *Women and Philanthropy in nineteenth-century England*, 1980, 169-70
22. Loius Blom-Cooper, *The Penalty of Imprisonment*, 1988, 6
23. Michael Ignatieff, *A Just Measure of Pain: The Penitentiary in the Industrial Revolution, 1750-1850*, 3
24. Elizabeth Fry, *op. cit.*, vol. 2, 387
25. Christopher Hibbert, *The Roots of Evil: a social history of crime and punishment*, 2003, 161
26. Michael Ignatieff, *op. cit.*, 78
27. Christopher Hibbert, *op. cit.*, 160
28. Michael Ignatieff, *op. cit.*, 207-215
29. Louis Blom-Cooper, *op. cit.* 10-11
30. *Ibid.*, 14
31. Frank Prochaska, *op. cit.*, 169
32. Harry Potter, *op. cit.*, 198-200
33. Stephen Tumim, *The Future of Crime and Punishment*, 1997, 45-50
34. Jo Deakin and Jon Spencer, 'Women behind bars: explanations and implications', *Howard Journal*, vol. 42, no. 2 (May 2003), 123-136, 123
35. Stephen Tumim, *op. cit.*, 52
36. Gordon Rose, *The Struggle for Penal Reform: The Howard League and its Predecessors*, 1961, 271-278

INDEX